THE
MENTALLY
TOUGH
COMPETITOR:
Mindsets and Perspectives to Be Your Best

BRIAN D. LOMAX, M.Ed.

CONTENTS

Introduction

In 2009, I started coaching tennis players on how to be mentally tougher. That was my side job. At the time, my profession was software testing, but I was unhappy in the corporate environment. I needed to do something on my own; something which was more meaningful to me than creating software for investors. By the summer of 2010, I was ready to go out on my own and I haven't looked back since.

Soon thereafter, I started writing blog posts about the mental game and how to compete better. Over time, the number of posts grew into the hundreds making it unwieldy for a visitor to the site to read all of them. With that in mind, I decided to create a collection of 50 posts based on three different themes: The Competitive Mindset, Competition & Performance, and Focus & Confidence. Each post, or chapter, has been updated to reflect my current thinking on the topic.

This book isn't meant to be a manual on Mental Toughness. That will come later. This book is about the mindsets and perspectives that can help you be mentally tougher. To be a great competitor, you have to be thinking right. You must view challenges, adversity, failure, success, character, motivation, focus, confidence, etc. in the right way. The way that allows you to move forward and improve. The way that allows you to embrace whatever comes along on your journey. If you can begin thinking right, the rest of mental toughness will come more easily.

As you go through this book, you can read the chapters in order, or you can jump around to topics that intrigue you. Whatever works for you. Some of the chapters have questions for you to answer, and you should take the time to do that. You'll get more out of this book if you clarify your thoughts in writing.

Enjoy.

-Brian Lomax

SECTION 1: THE COMPETITIVE MINDSET

1. MY JOURNEY TO MENTAL TOUGHNESS

When I was 6 years old, I failed advanced beginner swimming lessons. That was disappointing, and I was very upset, but it wasn't all bad. The silver lining was that it led to the beginning of my tennis career. At the time, my family had a membership at a swim and tennis club, and my two sisters and I went there on a daily basis. And as the name of the club implies, there were two basic activities one could do at this club: swim or play tennis. My reaction to failing at swimming lessons was to quit swimming altogether. Clearly, at this point in my life I didn't have the perspective of using failure as a learning opportunity! That would come much later.

With swimming no longer an option in my 6-year-old mind, I was left with tennis. It was the mid-1970's and the tennis boom was in full swing. I began to take lessons. I hit against a wall. I started to develop some proficiency, and since no one told me I was a failure, I continued to work. After a couple of summers of taking lessons, I began to compete on the club team and then in tournaments. As I got older, I started watching tennis on television more often and I became inspired by the stars of the era - players like Bjorn Borg and Ivan Lendl. I mimicked their serves, strokes, and mannerisms on the court (I didn't do so well mimicking their temperament though, but that's a story for another day!). I continued to improve and throughout my high school career, I was one of the best players in the state.

Sounds like a nice little story, doesn't it? The reality is that it's a story of unfulfilled potential for a couple of reasons. First, I resisted setting goals for my tennis career which meant that I had no vision of the type of player I wanted to become someday. I improved simply because I played a lot and I loved the sport, but my tennis growth wasn't as intentional as it could have been. If I had been more intentional about what I wanted from tennis, I would have worked harder on various parts of my game to reach my goals and I would be a far better player today.

Second, my reaction to losing and failure lacked perspective, and the behavior I exhibited as a 6-year-old, which was to quit when things got tough, continued throughout my teenage years. I would occasionally learn from losses, but I tended to see them as a validation of not being a good player rather than a stepping stone toward who I could become.

It wasn't until about age 30 that I started to develop some real mental toughness. At the time, I asked myself "Why didn't anyone tell me about this? Why didn't I know this before?"

This is why I started PerformanceXtra. I want people to know about these concepts. I don't want them to have to wait to find out about them like I did and then wonder why no one ever told them about this. There are many good athletes out there who have great potential, but they haven't learned how to be great competitors yet. They haven't had exposure to the information they need to become more intentional about their growth as a person and as an athlete. Being mentally tough and being a great competitor is something that just isn't taught today, and it truly should be. At PerformanceXtra, we have a system for training these skills and helping athletes reach their goals. If you're an athlete or a coach and you're serious about your sport, then I hope that you will find this collection of perspectives on the mental game helpful.

I want you to have the tools and information you need to be the best competitor or coach you possibly can be. I look forward to helping you on your journey.

2. THE POINT OF COMPETITION

What is the point of competition? The first thought that pops in your head is probably "winning!" However, that belief can be detrimental to performing one's best. In one of the cornerstone works of Positive Psychology, *Flow: The Psychology of Optimal Experience*, Mihaly Csikszentmihalyi writes that the point of competition is to provide an arena to perfect one's skill. That's an interesting perspective. He goes on to say that a sole focus on winning will eventually lead to a loss of enjoyment of competition. How many people do you know who have been on a losing streak at some point were simply not having fun playing their sport any longer? Perhaps you've experienced that, and perhaps we all have at some point.

Understanding that the point of competition is to perfect one's skills is a very process-oriented way of thinking and it supports the leap of faith that you need to make in order to become a better competitor. Remember that competition in itself is a life-long process. It's not just about today; it's about competition's role in your life over the course of many years. You're not always going to win, but you can always look to improve. Improve your skills and focus on the process, and trust that the results you want will come to you as a result of those skills getting better and better. Will you face some losses along the way? Absolutely, but that is another important element of competition – learn to fail or fail to learn. Losses and mistakes represent your best learning opportunities if you take the time to analyze them. They provide a road map for the skills you need to continue to improve in order for you to get better. Improve those skills and perhaps the next time you face that opponent, the result is better than the last time or possibly even goes in your favor.

To be a successful competitor in any sport, you must lose that fear of losing and making mistakes as it is a critical part of the learning process. I took a class in the summer of 2010 from the University of Pennsylvania on the Foundations of Positive Psychology, and the professor, Tal Ben Shahar, hammered "learn to fail or fail to learn" into our brains – in a good way of course! He used Thomas Edison's discovery of the light bulb as an example of learning from one's failures and applying those lessons to the next try. Edison didn't quit after the first failure, did he? No, he continued on and failed hundreds and possibly thousands of times before succeeding, but in the end, he did succeed and that's what we remember him for – the one success. Near the end of that particular lecture, the professor said something that sounded a bit odd at first, but upon reflection makes a lot of sense – "I wish you much failure on your journey through life". The more failure we experience, then the more you will learn. So, with inspiration from Dr. Tal Ben Shahar, I wish you many losses and mistakes in your future! Push the boundaries of your skills and expand them. Continue the learning process and trust that you'll be a better player and person for it.

3. THE 3 COMPONENTS OF MENTAL TOUGHNESS

I've given a lot of thought to Mental Toughness, and what it is and why we struggle with it. At a high level, there are 3 components to Mental Toughness in which athletes need a solid base in order to perform well. They are Philosophy, Character Skills, and Actions. Unfortunately, most athletes are deficient in one or more of these.

When you think of Mental Toughness, you probably relate more to Character Skills and Actions as that's what we can see (actions are based on one's character traits). However, one's Philosophy on competition, adversity, challenges, etc. is also important and that is where athletes normally are weakest. Let's explore these 3 components to understand them better.

Philosophy

The term Philosophy probably prompts you to think of the ancient Greeks and Romans, or Confucius and Lao-Tzu. Perhaps it reminds you of a boring class you took in high school or college. Whatever it is, you are probably not excited about this subject (kudos to you if you are!). What do these philosophers and other great thinkers have to do with mental toughness and being a great competitor? Quite a lot actually.

Philosophy helps us create a mental model of the world which we use to determine what is important and what isn't. From that, we develop mindsets and perspectives that allow us to develop the necessary character skills and actions that we need to become our best.

An example: From Stoicism, we learn that obstacles are actually the path to improvement rather than something to be avoided. Obstacles and adversity challenge us and therefore force us to be better if we want to be successful. If we adopt that philosophy, we can change our viewpoint on adversity and therefore handle it better in the future. Perhaps we even learn to embrace it. Putting this philosophy into action in competition enables us to face adversity in a calm and confident manner. It's normal. It's expected. It's what we need in order to be better. Powerful stuff!

That is simply one example. There are literally dozens more that we can apply to competition and life that would enable us to develop our optimal character and optimal actions. Make a commitment to developing your philosophy and you will see improvements in your performance in all areas. Here are some books to get you started on developing your personal philosophy:

The Four Agreements by Don Miguel Ruiz
The Greatest Salesman in the World by Og Mandino
Meditations by Marcus Aurelius
The Obstacle is the Way by Ryan Holiday

Character Skills

When thinking of Character Skills, I believe it's helpful to separate them into 2 categories: Ethical and Individual. Ethical traits represent how we treat and relate to others. Examples are integrity, respect, fairness, gratitude, and honesty. Individual traits represent how you relate to yourself, and examples include focus, discipline, creativity, confidence, persistence, resilience, love of learning, ambition, etc. Of course, there are many more examples in both categories and it's important to consider which character skills you want/need to develop in order to be a great competitor. Can you see how developing a Philosophy on competition could help you improve your definition of these character skills? The character skill of Resilience is directly related to the example in the Philosophy section above. It's much easier to be resilient if you view adversity as a normal and necessary component of improvement rather than something to avoid.

As human beings, we all have strengths and weaknesses and that applies to character skills as well. To discover your character strengths, visit http://www.viacharacter.org and take the free VIA Survey. Once you have the results, look for ways to use those strengths on a regular basis in competition and in your life. Maximizing strengths is a great way to take yourself to the next level.

Actions & Behaviors

The third piece of the Mental Toughness model is where the magic happens: Action. Your philosophy and character go nowhere if there is no action. In order for action to be effective, it must be intentional and with purpose. As human beings, we're taking "action" all day long, but does every action have a purpose? Are we acting with intention? This is the basic difference between activity and accomplishment.

In my work with athletes, I train them on the "actions of mental toughness." These are the actions that mentally tough competitors do in practice and competition regardless of how they feel. They also do them regardless of whether their competition is doing them or not. Examples are bouncing up and down, shaking out your arms to remove tension, breathing mindfully, having set routines, walking with confidence, etc. These actions need to be trained with the same diligence as the technical aspects of sport. Their purpose is to help your mind and body function better together which will help you to perform well on a more consistent basis. It's amazing what you can do when your mind is clear, your muscles are loose, and you feel confident and in control. Contrast that with how you feel today when you compete. There is probably a difference.

Of course, there are actions outside of competition and practice that can assist with overall performance, and this is why we need to study the process of performance. Making incremental improvements in different areas of the process will add up to big impacts in competition. For example, committing to 8 to 10 hours of sleep every night will have an impact on the quality of your days. Changes don't have to be huge, but they need to be consistent. Think of some small changes you could make in your life that would have an effect on how you compete.

As you continue on your competitive journey, use the 3 components of mental toughness as a framework to make improvements. The solutions to all of the performance barriers that you have are within these 3 components. For example, if you are struggling with nerves:

- Examine your philosophy/perspective on what you are getting nervous about
- Determine the character skills needed to succeed in this situation
- Commit to taking purposeful action that will be based on the first 2 components

This 3-step formula can help you overcome any barrier in your competitive career and make you the great competitor that you want to be.

4. WHERE MENTAL TOUGHNESS LIVES

One of my favorite books on mental toughness is *The Mindful Athlete* by George Mumford, because it reminds me of the importance of committing to a meditation practice on a daily basis. That daily practice allows me to be at my best more often. One of the benefits of mindfulness that I have come to appreciate is the ability to suspend judgment of an event, and then give myself time to look at it from multiple points of view before deciding on what I should do, if anything. This applies to not only athletic performance, but to life in general.

Oftentimes, people react immediately to what is going on around them with various emotions, and they become servants of those reactions. There is no space between stimulus (action, event, etc.) and response. There is no time to simply observe what is happening in the moment. That's a lost opportunity to experience more in the present moment. This is where Mental Toughness lives – the space between stimulus and response. When we don't take that moment between stimulus and response, we often take the experience personally and emotionally. Rarely are such events personal in nature. They most likely have nothing to do with us; they are just events. By seizing that moment before response, we can learn to not take things personally, and instead, develop an emotional awareness that allows us to mindfully choose how we want to feel in the present. Looking at an event from multiple points of view allows us to develop compassion and empathy for others. We can better understand why people do things when we are able to suspend judgment and put ourselves in the shoes of others.

Perhaps we may have reacted similarly in the past when faced with similar circumstances.

As an athlete, the ability to suspend judgment is critical to performing well, for emotional reactions often lead to sub-optimal performances. Former UCLA men's basketball coach John Wooden said, "Emotionalism destroys consistency." I agree with that statement. *Mental toughness lives in the gap between stimulus and response.* Instead of being ruled by emotions, the athlete must learn to interrupt the stimulus–response process and respond in such a way that is productive and beneficial to performing well. It's not easy to do this especially when there is a lack of mental discipline. That is why adding mindfulness to your training regimen is important; it is the consistent practice that develops mental discipline. It teaches you to slow down your mind, observe your own thoughts in a non-judgmental manner, and to maintain present focus.

Here are a few other thoughts to consider regarding emotionalism and the stimulus–response process:

- What is more important to you: being perfect or having a good overall performance? When you get emotional about mistakes, you are showing the world that the mistake you just made is more important to you than playing well, fighting, and winning. Is that how you want to present yourself?
- There is a difference between intensity and anger. Anger is undisciplined and unfocused. It is a waste of energy. Intensity is highly focused energy toward a goal. Some claim that they use anger to generate intensity. That can work, but it is a dangerous path. It is far more likely to lead to inconsistency. Instead, strive to create a calm intensity from your motivation, your goals, and your desire to succeed today.

An easy way to get started with meditation is through the use of guided meditations. There are many apps that can help you do this. With consistent effort, I am positive that you will see the benefits of mindfulness on your performances.

5. WHAT IS YOUR DEFINITION OF SUCCESS?

A few years ago, I spoke to a group of dressage instructors/trainers at an educational conference, and my topic was "How to be a Positive Coach." While I didn't have much credibility in the horse world, I do have a good bit of experience and knowledge on coaching styles in both sports and business. In this session, I knew I was preaching to the choir in terms of positive coaching, and so my goal was to get the trainers to think about how they could be more explicit in developing positive qualities in their programs and their students.

One of the fundamental questions that we considered as a group was "what is your definition of success?" Whenever I ask that question, I know the audience's immediate thoughts go to winning, trophies, ribbons, medals, money, fame, etc. Many of us have been programmed to think that way. We believe that rewards and status define success. Even though this is the immediate thought, it's rare that someone will actually say it, because deep down we know that it's not correct. It feels a bit shallow. There has to be a more meaningful definition, right?

Each person's definition of success is a very personal choice. I suggest that you write your own definition and be as specific as possible to your situation and/or your sport. If you choose to define success based on winning and results, know that those things are not under your direct control. You won't always win, and you won't always get the results you want. The odds are against us all that we'll become the best in the world in our chosen sport. Does that mean we are all failures? In my mind, it doesn't, but you may feel that way.

When a coach has a win at all costs attitude, the impact on his or her athletes can be profound. These coaches view their athletes as a means to achieve their personal desires for winning. It's not about developing the athlete as a person, but instead is all about the coach. In his book *InSideOut Coaching*, Joe Ehrmann refers to this type of coach as transactional. Transactional coaches won't hesitate to put moral and ethical values aside in order to attain results, as winning is the only thing that matters. That example teaches athletes to do the same and they often end up making similar decisions outside of sports. It's hardly surprising that we see so much cheating and corruption in sports, business and government. The notion that sport builds character is a myth.

As you ponder your own definition of success, consider incorporating these three concepts: effort, striving for your potential, and self-satisfaction. Notice that all three of these concepts are under your control. When I ask students or groups to write their own definition of success, I don't tell them about effort, potential, and self-satisfaction, but they almost always incorporate all three of them in their definition. The difficulty for many of us comes in adhering to this idealistic version of success in the face of a society obsessed with results. As a positive coach, it's my job to reinforce this definition with my students and to model it on a daily basis.

Once you've written your definition of success, compare it to John Wooden's definition. Wooden was famous for never talking to his team about winning yet his teams seemed to be quite adept at it (10 NCAA Men's Basketball championships). He's a great example of how you do not have to be a "win at all costs" type of coach in order to win.

"Success is peace of mind, which is a direct result of self-satisfaction in knowing you made the effort to do

your best to become the best that you are capable of becoming."

How did your definition compare to his?

6. A FORMULA FOR SUCCESS

Want a formula for being a successful competitor? Try this.

OPTIMISM * (PERSISTENCE + RESILIENCE) = SUCCESS

To understand this formula more completely, let's define our terms starting with Persistence and Resilience as they are the base elements in the equation. Persistence is the ability to sustain effort throughout a performance. We often see this as "not giving up" and giving your best effort at all times. You can't win consistently if your effort level varies within a performance and from event to event. It's a key ingredient in the competitive skill set.

Resilience is the ability to recover from adversity. It describes your ability to deal with mistakes, failures, losses and other negative events that may occur. As an athlete, you have to accept that some level of adversity will occur in competition and you need to be able to bounce back from that. It requires perspective. In general, you can't change what's already occurred, so you need to move on and direct your focus onto something you can control.

Both Persistence and Resilience are important character skills of great competitors and they work together. Watch any of the world's best competitors and you'll see them giving their best effort at all times, and they're ability to be resilient helps them continue that effort no matter what happens. When adversity does occur, they're able to move on quickly and refocus their efforts on what matters. Every athlete should work on improving these 2 skills. So how would you like to exponentially improve your persistence and resilience? Work on your Optimism.

Optimism is the tendency to expect a favorable outcome. In a competitive situation, it means you expect to win. You expect to be successful. The more optimistic you are, the more powerful your belief in the positive outcome. This type of self-belief is a key ingredient in achievement. Optimism drives self-belief. Self-belief drives achievement. Achievement drives increased Optimism.

Great competitors always believe they can win and they always believe they can play better when they are performing. That's the power of optimism. It raises your standard of excellence and it opens your eyes to achieving greater and greater things in your career.

In our success formula above, the multiplicative factor is Optimism. It can double, triple, or even quadruple your ability to persist and to bounce back. Over time that effect can be exponential. An easy way to understand the importance of this is to consider the effect of Pessimism on Persistence and Resilience. If you expect to lose or expect bad things to happen, your effort level suffers. What's the point of trying and bouncing back if you're going to lose anyway? There is no point, so you end up quitting mentally.

Optimism, Persistence and Resilience are key skills in mental toughness and being a great competitor. Use the formula above to take advantage of the power of Optimism to improve your Persistence and Resilience. Practice expecting the best possible outcome and you'll notice a difference in your results. When you see that difference, you'll drive your Optimism factor even higher.

7. THE SUCCESS FORMULA AT WORK

In the previous chapter, we reviewed the success formula:

SUCCESS = OPTIMISM * (PERSISTENCE + RESILIENCE)

In the Spring of 2013, there were some great examples of this in both the National Hockey League (NHL) and National Basketball Association (NBA) playoffs in which teams facing a seemingly insurmountable deficit were able to apply the success formula and emerge victorious. Let's start with hockey as the two teams who played for the Stanley Cup that year had their own comeback story.

The Boston Bruins were trailing 4-1 to the Toronto Maple Leafs with approximately 11 minutes remaining in the deciding game of their series. Then Bruins winger Nathan Horton got one back for the home team. From the Boston Globe (http://www.bostonglobe.com/sports/2013/05/13/bruins-stun-maple-leafs-game-thriller/aspCXWBFDAAa9Y9eUVsMzI/story.html):

"It was tough being on the bench, getting booed, looking up at the time clock, and watching those seconds count down," Brad Marchand said. "But after [David Krejci's] line got that first one for us and started to climb back, you could see the emotion on the bench. Guys started to believe. That's what we needed."

That belief, that optimism is what they needed to fuel the fighting spirit for the win. From that point on, the Bruins were in control of the game. They tied it up with seconds left in regulation and won the game six minutes into overtime.

In Chicago, the story was different, as the Blackhawks were trailing 3 games to 1 versus their hated rival the Detroit Red Wings. A series loss to Detroit would have been a crushing blow to the team that appeared so dominant for much of the regular season. After a loss in game 4, the Blackhawks held a team meeting which may have been the catalyst to their epic comeback. From ESPN (http://scores.espn.go.com/nhl/recap?gameId=400465772):

"We dug really deep," captain Jonathan Toews said. "We came in here and asked ourselves a question: How bad we wanted it. You got your answer right there. That's a heck of a way to pull out four wins in seven games."

Like the Bruins did in their series versus the Leafs, the Hawks went to overtime in game 7 to get their series victory. Toews' comment is insightful in that it refers to an appeal to the team's motivation and how bad they wanted it. Tapping into your motivation is a great way to make the Success Formula even more powerful.

Another example of an amazing comeback from the Spring of 2013 involved the Miami Heat and their game 6 victory over the San Antonio Spurs in the NBA Finals. Trailing by 5 points with 20 seconds remaining, Miami fans started streaming out of the arena believing their team would lose and that the Spurs would soon be celebrating another championship. Those fans, like most, didn't understand how elite athletes approach such situations and that they always have a belief that they can do something to pull out a victory. A 3-point shot from the Heat's Ray Allen with seconds to go in regulation sent the game into overtime and those fans who had left were pleading with arena security to let them back in the building. The Heat would go on to win by 3 in overtime.

What's the common thread in these 3 comebacks? Of course, the Success Formula is at work through Optimism, Persistence and Resilience, but at a more specific level, it's all about focusing on what you need to do in the moment. When the Bruins were trailing 4-1, the focus was to get just one goal, not 3. When they got that, then the focus was on getting another. And then another. The same process applied to the Blackhawks except for them, they needed the next game. And then the next. And then the next. In each of those games, the focus narrowed to getting the next goal. That's how you win. You don't win by trying to win. You win by focusing on the right things in the present moment. That process along with the Success Formula makes any athlete or team a great competitor.

8. THE ART OF UNLEARNING

Would you be surprised to learn that a major part of the process of becoming excellent is unlearning? Sure, learning new techniques is important, but the unlearning process addresses the habits and beliefs that limit your ability to reach true excellence. It is in this space that you can become truly elite.

One of my favorite episodes of the popular podcast, The Tim Ferriss Show is an interview with Josh Waitzkin. Josh was a chess prodigy as a child and the subject of the book and movie *Searching for Bobby Fischer,* and later became a world champion in Tai Chi. Josh wrote a book entitled *The Art of Learning* in which he explains his own journey to mastery of such disparate activities as chess and martial arts. Today, Josh works with a handful of elite performers and teaches them systems for maximizing their energy and creativity.

In the interview, Josh discusses a performer's tendency to judge situations as either good or bad, and how that judgment leads to mental, emotional and physical responses. To illustrate this, let's examine a situation in tennis that occurs: you lost the first set. It's likely that you judge this as a negative scenario in the match, and that in turn may affect your emotional state and alter your physiology away from its ideal condition. In this case, your judgment is harmful, but it is a habit that you have honed over the years. We tend to see things as good or bad, and that is the habit that we have to unlearn or upgrade.

What if you could change your perspective on losing the first set? I'm not suggesting that you should be happy that you lost it, but let's examine this differently. It is in these moments of adversity that true growth occurs. It is a challenge of your skills and if you embrace that moment, you will learn something about yourself. You will take your competitive skills to another level. It is all in your perspective. You must unlearn the habit of judging competitive situations, and instead replace that with an acceptance of what is happening in the moment. This is an opportunity to grow.

The Warrior Mindset describes one's ability to embrace the challenges of life. This concept is vital to any competitor's success. You want to ensure that you are viewing specific situations as challenges and growth opportunities rather than inherently "bad." While I've been using the term "unlearning" in this post, I'm not sure that's completely accurate from a cognitive perspective. I don't think we actually unlearn anything, but instead we replace or upgrade our skills and perspective. That's what we're doing here; we are upgrading our perspective on adversity so that we grow and improve from it. We take our skills to a new level and we continue to approach excellence. We don't shun adversity and react negatively. Instead, our upgraded perspective helps us realize that this adversity will make us stronger on our way to excellence. If excellence is what we truly want in life, then our actions must reflect that intention.

Coming back to Josh Waitzkin, he provides a simple example of the skill of judgment that needs an upgrade - the weather. From an early age, we are taught to view rain and snow as "bad" weather, and sunny as "good" weather. Is this actually the case? Think about it for a moment. Isn't it amazing that weather systems on this planet can create powerful forces like rain, snow, wind, etc.? Instead of viewing weather as good or bad, could we learn to appreciate it for what it is? OK, maybe we're getting kind of deep here, but the point is that our judgments determine our mental, physical and emotional reactions, and the weather is a simple means of understanding that. How many tennis players do you know who love the wind?

Once you upgrade your perspective on adversity in competition, you will be able to use your positive body language and breathing to compete better. These basic skills of mental toughness are more accessible when your perspective is focused on the path to excellence. Learn to be comfortable in the chaos of competition and you will have removed a major barrier in your journey to excellence.

9. TAKE ACTION TO TRANSFORM YOURSELF

One of the missions of a coach is to help athletes transform their games so that they become better players in the long term. In order for this to happen, we need to understand the difference between information and transformation. Let's use a simple example to illustrate this.

Imagine that you have never played a particular sport before and you are eager to learn. You decide that the first thing you want to do is read a book about how to play that sport. So you do that. You read the book, you study the pictures and diagrams, and perhaps you even view a DVD that came with the book. Now you have a lot of information on how to play the sport. You know what the game looks like, the various moves required, the necessary footwork. Can you actually play the sport? No. Can you go out and execute any of the high-level skills needed to play this sport? No. All you have is information.

How do you take this information and use it to create transformation? Simple – you take action, or in more common terminology for sports, you practice. Without action, information does nothing with respect to performance and over time that information may even be forgotten. By adding action and practice, you take advantage of neuroplasticity – the ability of the brain to actually transform based on what we learn and how we practice. When we first attempt a new skill, we create new neural pathways and the more we practice these new skills, the deeper and thicker those pathways become.

The reason for highlighting this topic is that this concept is often forgotten when learning about the mental aspects of sport. It's extremely important to remember that mental techniques need practice just as much as the physical skills. In both areas, you are trying to create automatic behavior and you can't do that without practice and repetition. Using a concept like The Reset Button (forgetting the past and focusing on the present) takes a lot of practice, and I mean a lot! Trying it once and having success with it doesn't mean you have the technique down cold. What you have done is formed a new neural pathway that needs a lot more repetition before it can become a habit and a strength of your game. And just as you do with your physical game, you're going to have ups and downs with the mental skills you are learning. That's not a reason to abandon them though as ups and downs are completely normal in performance.

The lesson is that if you want to be a better player and athlete, you have to practice the new skills and techniques that you are learning so that you can transform your game. Use the power of action to take information and create transformation.

10. PRESSURE MAKES YOU BETTER

I've missed over 9,000 shots in my career.
I've lost almost 300 games.
26 times I've been trusted to take the game-winning shot and
missed.
I've failed over and over and over again in my life.
And that is why I succeed.
- MICHAEL JORDAN

This quote from Michael Jordan is familiar to most and it highlights his own understanding that failing is part of the learning process, and without failure there can be no success. Even though the topic of this quote seems to be about failure, how do we remember Michael Jordan? We remember the game winning shots, the numerous championships and the many great performances. It's not only about failure leading to success. It's deeper than that. Michael Jordan wasn't afraid to fail in the big moment. He played to win, and he played with no regrets. He loved the pressure moments.

A few years ago, I asked a group of young tennis players what they thought the mindset of the top pros was in pressure situations. I was asking this question because about 80% of these young athletes feared the pressure moments of a match, and so I wanted to see if they had observed different behavior from the sport's best. The answer I heard from one young player was remarkable. He said, "the top players see pressure as an opportunity to prove themselves." I was stunned and asked him if I could quote him on that because he was right on.

The top athletes in the world don't fear pressure moments, they embrace them. They enjoy them because that's what competition is all about. Whether they experience success or failure in that moment, it's an opportunity to learn about themselves and further their skills as a competitor. To become a great competitor, you have to want to experience these moments or else you'll never reach your full potential. You will be denying yourself a tremendous learning opportunity. In a post-match interview from the 2012 Australian Open, Novak Djokovic expressed gratitude for his fellow competitors, namely Roger Federer and Rafael Nadal, for making him a better player because they forced him to learn how to earn major titles.

Young athletes don't like making mistakes and they certainly don't like losing. And because of that, they often play it safe or conservatively. In a team sport, you may see them hanging out on the fringe of play and never really getting involved. In an individual sport, they are similarly risk averse and build their whole performance around "no mistakes". In order to help these athletes, we have to encourage risk taking and when they inevitably make a mistake, discuss the mistake in the context of learning and getting better. Sports are like a giant laboratory for learning. We try things out, see what works and doesn't work, and try again. Sounds a lot like the rest of life, doesn't it? If we can make this learning process enjoyable, we can help create many more great competitors.

11. MOTIVATION: WHY DO YOU COMPETE?

Why do you compete? Why is your sport important to you?

Your answers to these questions can be quite revealing in terms of your desire to succeed, and whether or not you're ready to do what it takes to reach your potential. That's why motivation is one of the key ingredients in becoming a great competitor. It gives purpose and direction to your work. It is what keeps you going when adversity inevitably appears. Motivation is what drives you to continually improve and be the best athlete and competitor possible. Look at all of the greatest competitors in the world and you will see that they are constantly trying to get better. They are always trying to win more. For them, it's not about the money. It's about why they compete, and they all know the answer to that question.

There are two characteristics of motivation that I would like to discuss:

    1.Purpose
    2.Goals

Purpose

So why DO you compete? The usual quick answers are responses like "it's fun", "I like winning", "I'm good at it", etc. And because these are the quick answers that don't take much thought, they aren't very inspiring. They aren't the answers that are going to get you to practice on those days that you just don't feel like it. They aren't the answers that will help you push through adversity in your career. It's important to develop your purpose and it requires some thought. Spend some time considering the following questions:

- What do you like about competing?
- Who are you becoming because you are a competitor?
- What would your life be like if you didn't have competitive sport in it?
- How does your sport help you relate to other people and why is that important?
- What does success in your sport mean to you?

After you have answered these questions thoughtfully, revisit them once a week for a few weeks and see how your thinking evolves. Bring more consciousness to the meaning and purpose of your sport in your life, and how it is shaping you as a person and competitor.

Goals

Having a goal is important for everyone, as you need to set some target or destination for yourself if you want to reach your potential. As Yogi Berra said, "If you don't know where you're going, you might end up someplace else." I've experienced that personally, so I can tell you that there's a tremendous difference between working toward a goal and simply taking life as it comes. Chances are you'll improve at whatever you do either way, but you'll get better faster if you have a goal to work toward.

Once you have set a goal for yourself, one of the first things you want to do is think about who you need to be in order to achieve that goal. For example, let's say you want to be the starting quarterback for a Division I college football team. In order to do that, you need to start acting like a starting QB on a Division I college football team. That means adapting the habits and mindset of those that have already achieved that position. What's their schedule like? What are their workout routines? How do they eat? Who do they spend time with? What do they study? Who are their mentors and coaches? Start answering these types of questions for your goal and you'll start defining who you need to become. Start adapting the answers to these questions and you will have an excellent chance of becoming that person and reaching your goal.

When you have purpose and goals, you have the inspiration necessary to approach your full potential. Along that journey, there will be moments that require you to get out of your comfort zone and change how you do things. Having a well-developed motivation will allow you to break out of that comfort zone and do whatever it takes to become a great competitor. Enjoy that journey and fulfill your purpose.

12. PLAYING TO WIN

Have you ever watched a game in which the team that was leading stopped playing to win in favor of protecting their lead? And what usually happens in this situation? The team that is just protecting the lead ends up losing it. In football, we see this phenomenon with the "prevent" defense. In hockey and soccer, it often occurs when one team has a two-goal lead. In the 2013 NHL playoffs, there was a classic example of this in the Montreal Canadiens vs. the Ottawa Senators series in Game 4. The Canadiens had a 2-0 lead going into the 3rd period and went into "lead protection mode." Fast forward to the end of the game - Senators win 3-2 in overtime. For the first half of the 3rd period, Montreal could only generate one shot on goal while giving up nearly 10. It's no wonder they gave up the lead.

What is happening when teams or athletes protect a lead and let their opponents back in to the game? It's rather simple actually. It's the difference between playing to win and playing not to lose. Of course, everyone is familiar with those two concepts, but what may not be familiar is why athletes are in either play to win mode or play not to lose mode, and that comes down to whether there appears to be something to gain or something to lose.

When a team has the lead, the natural inclination is to begin to think about that lead and how they don't want to relinquish it. They want to protect it. The lead becomes more valuable than the win. Their focus has shifted to loss prevention, and loss prevention leads to poorer performance. When you try not to make mistakes, you invariably make more mistakes. On the flip side, the team that is trailing begins to realize that they don't have anything to lose and instead have everything to gain. They relax, they play more aggressively, take more risks and very often get back in the game. It's a simple difference between viewing a situation as something to gain versus something to lose.

The lesson is to realize that these forces are at work and that you can change this default behavior. When you have a lead, don't think about what you have to lose. Continue to think about what you have to gain. Remind yourself to play to win at all times because that's when you play your best. We almost never perform our best when we're playing not to lose. The prevent defense and protecting a lead in hockey or soccer are recipes for heartache. Those strategies may pay off at times, but a superior strategy is to keep playing your best by playing to win! Keep up the intensity and finish off your opponents. That's what great competitors do.

13. FEELING PRESSURE? GET EXCITED!

As a competitor, it's a certainty that you get nervous from time to time, both before you play and during competition. Fear is the emotion that drives nerves. Why is this? What are you afraid of? I decided to ask a group of junior tennis players what they were afraid of on the court and their answers were revealing:

- Losing
- Losing to a player who wasn't as good
- What their parents would think of them after a loss
- What other people would think of them after a loss
- Loss of reputation
- Playing in front of a coach
- Choking in a pressure situation
- Ranking going down
- The lecture in the car on the way home
- Playing badly and looking bad

What do all of these have in common? They are all negative outcomes, and when these types of thoughts are predominant in your mind, you will likely play with fear. Of course, a certain level of nervousness is good - it shows that you care - but we have to control it and keep our thoughts within the bounds of reality. If it's before the match, none of these negative outcomes has actually occurred yet, so why are you fixated on these? Well, we know that focusing on negative outcomes is part of our survival response as human beings, but our lives aren't under threat on the tennis court, so aren't more positive outcomes also possible? Yes! And we need to learn how to redirect our thoughts to WHAT WE WANT, and away from WHAT WE DON'T WANT (unfortunately, the lecture in the car will probably happen no matter what).

Conventional wisdom tells us that when we are experiencing fear in competition that we should attempt to calm ourselves down, but that's the wrong answer. Moving from a "high arousal/energy" state like nervousness to a "low arousal/energy" state like calmness doesn't aid performance. Instead, we want to use this high arousal/energy state and channel our emotions from Fear to Excitement.

Sounds easy enough, but how can you do it? Here are 4 things to incorporate into your preparation and performances.

1. Fix your relationship with pressure and challenges: Pressure and challenges are actually what make you a better player as you need them to improve. They test your skills. Get excited about getting better today. Embrace the pressure!
2. Write / think of all of the positive outcomes that could occur: Improvement, play well, win, improve ranking, going for ice cream after the match, reach a goal, etc.
3. Take action: Mental Toughness is an action first so start moving your feet, bouncing up and down, walking with confidence and energy, etc. As you are doing this, think of your best performances. Visualize playing your best today. Do this before you play, and more importantly, while you are competing. Be consistent with this throughout your performance.
4. Use music and video to inspire you. Have a favorite player? Watch him/her for 5 or 10 minutes. Use a

pump-up playlist and visualize playing your best while listening to it.

Like any skill in life, this takes practice and it's a process. We'll never completely get rid of the fear - and we don't necessarily want to - but we can use more productive emotions such as excitement, confidence, optimism and positivity to fuel our performances. Use the 4 steps above to keep moving yourself in the right direction.

14. SUCCESS AND CONSISTENCY

When you hear the word consistency, what images come to mind? If you're a tennis player, you'll most likely imagine someone who never misses a shot. In basketball, it might be a player with a high free throw percentage. Whatever it is you imagine, it is only a very small part of what being consistent means in the overall scheme of becoming a successful athlete and competitor.

Consider being more consistent with your efforts in the following areas:

- Preparation
- Focus and Concentration
- Effort within your performance
- Strength Training
- Practice
- Footwork
- Watching the ball, puck, etc.
- Breathing and Relaxation
- Routines
- Positive attitude
- Sleep
- Nutrition
- Goal Setting
- Motivation and Inspiration

That's a long list and it would be safe to say that I have not covered everything involved in the process of being a great competitor. However, consider what appears above and evaluate the consistency of your own effort in these areas. The ultimate goal is for you to design a daily and weekly agenda that will lead to better and better performances over time. It's often said in the business world that one's success can be determined by one's daily agenda. What's on your daily and weekly agenda? Is it consistent enough? Is everything on it helping you reach your goals and attain your best performances?

Keep a log of what you do every day for 2 weeks and then revisit these questions. You will probably be surprised by the amount of time or activities that have nothing to do with you getting better at what is important in your life. If you can redesign what you do every day based on being consistent in the areas listed above, you will transform your life and take a giant leap toward your ultimate potential.

15. BE MORE POSITIVE

One of the fundamental aspects of the PerformanceXtra program is to be more positive in competition, in your training and in your life in general as this has been proven to be a determinant for success. To most people, that sounds fairly logical. However, there is a lot of literature that misrepresents what being positive really means and whether it is truly beneficial to performance, so let's talk about "being more positive."

You may read books or articles in which being positive is presented as being unrealistic. According to these sources, positive thinking is simply thinking that only positive things can and will happen, while ignoring all negative thoughts. They may then go on to extoll the virtues of negative thinking and even equate being negative with being realistic.

Why is negative thinking considered to be realistic while positive thinking is viewed as fantasy? Do good things happen in life? Yes, they do, and the same is true for bad things. Isn't reality a mix of positive and negative? This is where I think some people choose to represent positive thinking as it's presented in a work like *The Secret*, which is all about just thinking good thoughts and letting good things happen to you, rather than a more scientific work from Positive Psychology like *Positivity* by Barbara Frederickson. From this discrepancy, it is clear that we need a better definition of what is positive and what isn't.

Frederickson's book *Positivity* discusses the necessary ratio of positive to negative thoughts to be successful in life. The minimal ratio for flourishing in life is 3 positive thoughts to 1 negative and she shows how this has been proven both qualitatively through surveys as well as quantitatively through elaborate mathematical equations. Notice that there is a negative thought involved in that 3 to 1 ratio. It isn't 3 to 0.

That's because Positive Psychology is reality based. It's not a formula for becoming a pollyanna. Reality is a mixture of the positive and the negative.

In a previous chapter, I introduced a formula for success:

Success = Optimism*(Persistence + Resilience)

If I truly believed that all you needed to do was think positive thoughts and everything would be great, then I could have simplified my formula to Success = Optimism or Success = Positivity. But I didn't do that because I don't believe that's true. Success takes hard work and a lot of it. That's the Persistence part. On the road to success, you will encounter obstacles. How you handle them is Resilience. Those two factors embrace the reality of life. Having a positive mental attitude can exponentially help you with these two important character traits.

What exactly do I mean by a positive thought versus a negative thought? My simple definition is that a positive thought allows you to do something constructive while a negative thought either provides no plan of action or a destructive one. You are either thinking constructively or you are not. When we compete, it's important to be thinking constructively even if the tone of your private voice is negative or critical. The next time you compete, examine your own thoughts and determine whether they are constructive or not. And don't be afraid to be more positive and optimistic out there! It will help you to be successful in every aspect of your life.

16. BEING MENTALLY TOUGH IS TOUGH!

Let's face it - being mentally tough in competition is difficult. One of the reasons for that is the many apparent contradictions as to what to do and what to focus on in a given moment. There are no black and white answers that tell you to focus on just this one thing or do this one thing and you'll be fine. There is a lot of gray area involved and it's difficult to find the right balance of what to do and what to focus on.

For example, it is important to understand the long-term goal of playing well and winning (hopefully), yet at the same time focusing on the moment and giving your best effort. Too much focus on winning can hurt performance because it might induce fear and nerves. Not enough focus on that overall goal could cause you to make bad decisions from moment to moment. A balance between the two is required, and that takes practice and experimentation which will build experience.

Another apparent contradiction for tennis players is the notion that some points are more/less important than others. While that is true, the message is not that you should play "less" important points with less effort than other points. You always want to give your best effort on every point, but the key is to manage your reaction once the point is over so that you don't take yourself out of the match. In sports like tennis and volleyball, you almost always have a chance to recover from a lost point, but you need to bring your best game to each one when the next point is in front of you.

The key to dealing with these contradictions is to first be aware that they exist. There are nuances and gray areas to the mental game, and that's ok. Accept it. Many athletes don't recognize this and therefore, they under-perform when the pressure mounts. They may learn this concept over time through experience or they may never learn it at all. One of the first steps for you to become a great competitor is to realize that this isn't easy and it's going to take some dedicated practice to learn to compete better.

Next, you'll have to specifically train these skills with a goal of making yourself an extremely calm and highly rational competitor who makes great decisions all the time. Because these are new skills, it will be difficult and exhausting at first. You'll be putting a lot of mental energy into this process and you probably won't get into the zone while you're playing. But once you are able to reconcile these apparent contradictions through deliberate practice and experience, you'll establish patterns of thought that will no longer need to be consciously called under pressure. They will become instinctual to your performance and part of your identity as a competitor. And then you will be more able to get into the zone because you will have quieted your mind and let your new patterns of thought go on auto-pilot.

17. DEALING WITH THE EXPECTATIONS OF WINNING

"I should beat that guy."
"We should beat them."

The above are statements that we have all made in our lives as competitive athletes and in many cases, we were probably correct in our assessment of the match up. Of course, there are games and matches in which we are the favorites and we should absolutely win. However, such statements can be detrimental to overall performance if you don't have the mindset of a great competitor. I bet you've lost one or more of these games or matches in which you said this. I know I have.

When an athlete says "I / We should win", what happens in the athlete's mind? Frankly, this isn't a particularly productive statement. Nothing good happens as a result of you saying this whether it's true or not. First, it puts added pressure on you to achieve a victory – as if you didn't have enough pressure already! You have declared to the world that you are supposed to win – what will happen if you don't? This added pressure can affect your performance in a negative way especially if things don't go well. You may begin thinking "how can this be happening, I should be beating this guy" or other similarly non-productive thoughts. You begin to tighten up. You start making bad decisions. Fear becomes the dominant emotion and your body chemistry begins to reflect that – high heart rate, jittery and/or tight muscles, frustration, etc. Instead of playing your best against an opponent you should beat, you end up playing and competing poorly. And unfortunately, you have no one to blame but yourself.

Additionally, the statement "I should win" could be construed as being disrespectful to the opponent as it suggests that you don't need to be at your best to win. Let's address the respect factor first. Everyone who has the courage to compete deserves your respect. It takes guts to go out there and put oneself on the line knowing that losing is a distinct possibility. This is especially true in the internet age in which for many sports, results are posted online for all to see. Think of how many people are afraid to compete in anything in life and you'll automatically have more respect for those who do. Respect your opponents regardless of their ability level for they are courageous.

One way to show respect to your opponents is to give them your best effort at all times. If you don't respect them, you may believe that you can get away with less than your best effort and that often leads to a lack of focus on the important factors in your performance. For all you know, your opponent has been working really hard in practice and may even have a specific game plan just for you and/or your team.

So how should we handle the "I / We should win" statement? In an ideal situation and from the mindset of a great competitor, we should try to eliminate this statement from our thoughts. Opponents are obstacles for us regardless of their ability. Our job is to focus on our best performance, compete hard and learn from the experience. Then we tackle the next opponent. It is a mindset in which we acknowledge that if we are not at our very best we could lose to anyone. This is the type of language that you hear from the best competitors in the world like Rafael Nadal.

Eliminating "I / We should win" from your vocabulary is easier said than done and like anything it's a process. When these thoughts come to mind (and they probably will), your reaction to them must shift from one of creating pressure and expectations for yourself to one of taking control of the situation. How do you do that? When you say "I should win" add something like the statement below to the end of that sentence.

"I SHOULD WIN THIS MATCH, BUT I'LL NEED TO GIVE MY BEST EFFORT AND FOCUS TO BE SUCCESSFUL."

You could certainly add more detail to the second half of the sentence in terms of what you need to do to be successful as that is what is important. But notice what we've done in this sentence. We have inserted the mindset of a great competitor into the second part of it. That mindset allows us to take control over the situation because we are stating what we are going to do. It's process focused. The first part of the sentence is result focused and is something that we don't have total control over.

If you can add these types of thoughts to "I / We should win", you will eventually be able to eliminate even using that phrase in the first place. And you will have taken a huge leap in your journey toward being a great competitor.

18. BE A LEADER

Leadership is an important quality for many of us whether we are players, captains, coaches or managers. We want to be good leaders. But what does a good leader do? Is it all about winning or is there more to it than that?

If you're an aspiring leader, think about taking your leadership skills to a level that transcends just winning. Winning in itself doesn't imply that you did it the right way. However, if you're a great leader - a transformational leader - not only will you be successful, but you'll be remembered for making those around you better. That sounds like a pretty cool legacy to me. What do you think?

Do you want to be a great leader? Here are 4 things to add to your leadership toolbox so that you can be a transformational leader.

Always do the right thing

As a leader, you have to model the behavior you wish to see in others. In a sports context, that means always giving your best effort, being fully focused and engaged in practice and in games, putting the team ahead of yourself, being respectful, and displaying great sportsmanship in all situations. I'm sure you can come up with a few more items to add to this list. The key is to model that behavior, as your actions will speak louder than your words.

Inspire others

When you communicate with your teammates or players, share the vision of what your team can be and what it can accomplish if everyone does the necessary work. Make that vision inspiring and appealing to all. Praise others for their hard work, commitment, dedication, and stay away from telling people how talented they are without connecting it to effort. Strive to make those around you better by inspiring them with a grand vision.

Engage on an intellectual level

When you're away from practice or competition, do you talk about your sport? You should. I'm not saying that you should never talk about anything else, but you want to engage your teammates and players in intellectual discussions on your sport so that collectively, you can all raise your sport IQ. Smarter teams win. That means understanding strategy, tactics, the tendencies of opponents, technical skills, the history of the game, etc. Talk about this stuff on a regular basis. That's what great leaders and teams do.

Show them you care

Get to know all of your teammates and players, and learn about what is important in their lives. We don't want to view them simply as a means to an end (i.e., I just need you so we can win this game). There will be times when our teammates are struggling outside of sport, and it's in those moments that we can reach out and offer assistance to them. Help them celebrate their personal triumphs. Let them know that being on the team goes beyond just performing on the court or on the field. You care about them as human beings and you want them to be successful in all things that are important in their lives.

There are coaches who win and don't do these 4 things or place much importance on them. The media and the history books may remember them for their success, but their players will most likely look back on them in a different way. They'll note that the relationship was distant or empty, and if they learned anything about human relations in the process, it was more on the side of what not to do. Contrast that with the praise that players heap on former UCLA basketball coach, John Wooden. His teams were successful because he made his players better men, and through that process, they learned how to reach their potential as a team.

As an athlete who aspires to leadership, you can do the same 4 things noted above. And by doing so, you'll develop lifelong relationships that will be mutually enriching. While John Wooden is a great example of a transformational leader, there are many more out there. Research those in your sport and use them as role models for developing your leadership style.

19. RESPECT AND SPORTSMANSHIP

On New Year's Day in 2015, the University of Oregon and Florida State University (FSU) played in a College Football Playoff game at the Rose Bowl in Pasadena, California. Oregon won the game handily, 59-20. At the end of the game, a large number of the players from FSU walked off the field without shaking hands and congratulating their opponents. The TV announcers observed this and commented on it. Fan reaction on Twitter and social media was not favorable toward those players as it was deemed to have demonstrated a lack of grace on the part of the FSU football program.

The day after this incident, I came across an article written by a sport psychologist who had a different take on the incident. In his view, athletes should not be compelled or forced to shake hands at the end of a contest if they don't want to do that. Of course, he'd prefer that they did, but forced handshakes don't teach sportsmanship. I agree. Look at any line of Little League baseball players shaking hands and you'll see the majority of them not even looking at the players on the other team. Occasionally, we'll see this from pro tennis players when they come together at the end of a match. There is neither interest nor recognition of the opponent by these athletes in both victory and defeat.

While forced handshakes don't necessarily teach sportsmanship, as a coach, I don't believe that the conversation should stop there. Why don't those athletes want to shake hands at the end of a contest? It's a question that needs to be asked and discussed, for without those opponents, athletes cannot achieve anything. Sure, they may be upset that they lost or at the way they played. Maybe the opponent cheated, or the officials blew a call. Being upset and disappointed is understandable and the emotions are valid, but it lacks perspective when it comes to the nature of competition.

If forcing handshakes doesn't teach sportsmanship, then what does? It starts with respect. Respect for yourself. Respect for your teammates, coaches, officials, parents, fans, and yes, your opponents. In their book *True Competition*, David Light Shields and Brenda Light Bredemeier refer to opponents as our "partners" in the quest to fulfill our potential in the realm of competition. Without opponents, we cannot achieve our peak performances. Without opponents, we don't learn about ourselves. We need them, and they need us. And while we all want to win, we are also helping each other get better by giving our best effort and being the best that we can be every day. Every day that we compete is a learning experience.

If you're a coach and you want to engender sportsmanship into your program, teach your athletes how to exercise and flex the character muscle of respect for themselves and for others. Teach them that winning today is not as important as reaching their full potential in the future, and that they need others to help them fulfill that dream. Have your athletes come up with ideas for how they can demonstrate more respect. You'll be pleasantly surprised at all the good ideas they come up with in this exercise. Make it a core value of your program, model it yourself, and you'll build good sportsmanship in your athletes.

20. ARE YOU A PERFECTIONIST?

In my work with athletes, I encounter a lot of perfectionists. I don't know if this is more prevalent in today's society than in the past, but it seems as if there is now a romantic ideal associated with being a perfectionist. Like it is a good thing. Like being a perfectionist is a badge of honor. I'm not so sure it is a good thing. In fact, I'm certain it isn't especially if you're an athlete who wants to become a great competitor. Or simply great at anything. Perfectionism is a barrier. Perfectionism will slow your progress and likely make you miserable in the process.

With that being said, perfectionism does have a positive side: high standards. It can be a force for us to seek excellence in our lives and the desire to achieve great things. That's good stuff! However, the problem with perfectionism begins with the journey toward the goal. Most perfectionists dislike the idea of making mistakes on the path to their goal and end up hating the journey. Unfortunately, reality is filled with imperfect moments. Mistakes are a part of life and a necessary part of the learning process. So, if you're a perfectionist, guess what? You're not a realist.

At some point in life, a human being's relationship with making mistakes changes. As babies and young children, we don't worry about making mistakes and instead channel our energy into the effort of improving a skill. For example, take walking. Ever see a young child attempt to walk for the first time, fall down and then never try again? Of course not. A baby isn't worried about how mistakes make him/her feel or how he/she looks to others because of a failure, but instead cares more about learning to walk. That baby will try and try and try until he's walking. There's a lesson for us in how a baby handles falling down, and it is one of perspective. What is more important: learning the skill or living up to some image you have created for yourself and others? The baby values the skill.

At some point later in our cognitive development, we begin to associate making mistakes to our own self-image and how others perceive us. Those factors become more important to us than any learning that may occur via making mistakes, and thus the experience becomes emotional. We don't like what making mistakes says about us as a person. Therein lies the barrier to greatness.

Bringing this back to sports, perfection isn't usually a necessary requirement for being successful. In fact, in a sport like tennis, the scoring system allows you to make mistakes and lose points with no major consequences in the overall result. For example, if I lose the first point of the first game of a match, have I really lost anything of significance? No. I can easily recover from that. Additionally, if I lose the first game of the match, I can easily recover. The objective is to win sets. Points and games add up to sets, but we have to keep them in perspective. Unfortunately, many tennis players are not skilled in doing this and instead become emotional about mistakes and lost points. That's part of the journey of a tennis match!

Of course, there are some sports in which the standard of perfection is valued more highly such as figure skating, gymnastics and dressage, but being a perfectionist in training isn't the path to greatness in those endeavors either. Mistakes are valuable and if you commit the right kind of mistakes - going for it versus holding back - you will find that they are a gateway to mastery.

To help deal with perfectionism, we must understand that making mistakes and losing does not mean we are failures. Remember why you play your sport. It shouldn't be about winning only, but rather about discovering how good you can actually become. That's in your control. Mistakes are part of the learning process and the more good mistakes you make, the more of your potential will be revealed.

Personally, I have struggled with this concept as a tennis player, but I have made positive strides in using good mistakes (especially in practice) as a way of moving my game forward. I need to do it more though because I feel as if I can still get better. How about you? Can you commit to making more good·mistakes to see how good you can become?

21. MENTAL TOUGHNESS WISDOM FOR THE TENNIS PLAYER

Even though the title of this chapter refers to tennis players, I believe any athlete can gain perspective from these ten points. Apply them and reap the benefits.

1. When your opponents make excuses for why they lost to you, take it as a compliment. You broke them mentally and now they're desperate to protect their self-esteem. It proves that you ARE the mentally tougher player.
2. Regardless of the score, look at every point as an opportunity to break your opponent mentally. How you perceive each moment is your choice. Choose to have a productive perspective.
3. Write down five reasons why you are tough to compete against. Once you have that list, commit to doing those things more often when you practice and play.
4. Most athletes don't treat their minds like muscles and therefore have undisciplined thoughts and beliefs. This can improve with training, but you have to be open minded about doing the necessary work that brings about more discipline and control. If you think that your mind simply works a certain way and there is nothing to be done about it, then your

mental game will not progress. Be coachable! Get yourself into a "mind gym."

5. It's okay to be irrationally optimistic when competing – it might win you a match. Being pessimistic won't win you anything so why would you choose that? It's shocking how many players choose pessimism over optimism.

6. Your goal should not be to win points, but instead to play great points. Play enough great points and the winning will happen. The question is, do you know how to play a great point?

7. Your best performances go through your strengths so go to them under pressure.

8. Part of deliberate practice is practicing competing.

9. Always respect your opponents. You need them. No one can create a great tennis match by himself/herself. Your opponent is also your partner.

10. Every tennis player has three roles on the court: the player, the coach, and the official. Your training should address all three of these.

What are your thoughts on these? Can you apply them to your game?

SECTION 2 –
COMPETING &
PERFORMANCE

22. DID YOU KNOW THAT COMPETING IS A SKILL?

If you are an athlete who has ever had to come back from an injury, you realize that the hardest part is getting back to your level of play in a tournament or competitive environment. After practicing for a while, your technique may feel like it used to, but the first time you decide to compete, your game just isn't there. Frustration ensues, and you wonder what is going on.

WHAT IS GOING ON??? The reality is that competing is a set of skills, and those skills need to be sharpened just as much as your physical game if you are to return to your competitive level as quickly as possible. I've had to learn this the hard way. In my career, I've had several major injuries resulting in layoffs of 3+ months, and I feel as if I'm an expert on how to come back. If only I could become an expert at staying healthy rather than pushing myself to a complete physical breakdown!

When you first return to competition, realize that the following skills may not be at the level they were prior to your injury:

- Focus
- Decision making
- Confidence
- Breathing
- Time management
- Mindset under pressure

Without these skills, it will be difficult for your physical game to succeed in competitive situations so be patient with the process. As you practice and compete, work on these skills more consciously by setting process goals that support them. For example, I might combine focus and time management into one goal such as "use my in-between points routine consistently and always reset to a next point mentality." Sharpening those two skills allows me to play one point at a time and that's a big part of my mental game. If I didn't work on those two skills, I might get too emotional about past mistakes and let those affect my thinking going into the next point. Then 0-15 becomes 0-40 and I am wondering, "how did I get here?" Let the downward spiral of frustration begin!

A few years ago, I remember coming back from an injury and playing my first competitive tennis in over 5 months with the express purpose of practicing my competitive skills. In that regard, it was a success. I managed to win a couple of matches mainly because I was better at the competitive skills than my opponents and I didn't get frustrated with myself. It was a lot of work, but eventually I got back to my pre-injury level of play, and maybe even a bit better. Working on the competitive skills was the difference.

As you design your comeback plan, budget time for training your competitive skills in a conscious and patient manner. You'll find the process to be much less frustrating and you will probably find your top competitive game even sooner than you normally would.

23. DO YOU WANT TO WIN?

Do you like to win? Of course, you do. Perhaps you think that's a silly question for me to pose, but what if I told you that while most athletes say they want to win, their behavior often says something entirely different. It says that mistakes and being perfect are more important to them than winning. Their focus isn't fully on the long-term goal; it's stuck in the past. Because of that, they aren't able to perform their best throughout the competition.

Let's use the sport of tennis to illustrate this behavior as its scoring system is particularly devilish. With a winner and loser on every single point, tennis players often fall into the trap of judging themselves based on the result of a point. Players may react emotionally and/or lose focus because of this. They become concerned with something they can't change (the past) and therefore they bring less energy to what is in their control (the next point). Their behavior says that they care more about the past, and that winning the match is a lower priority. Most players think that the desire to be perfect and the desire to win go hand-in-hand. They don't.

The total number of points won in a tennis match does not determine the winner, and neither does the total number of games. Winning sets is what matters, and therefore it is not necessary to win every single point. When you realize this and stop judging yourself after every point, you come to understand that the tennis scoring system is actually quite forgiving. It allows you to lose points with no real consequences on the scoreboard. How great is that?! You don't have to be perfect! Lose a point – so what? Simply play better on the next one. The next point is always an opportunity to play better.

Getting comfortable with this perspective takes time, and so I want to show you two lists of behaviors that demonstrate what you value more while you are competing. These behaviors represent the extremes and you may see that you display behaviors from both lists at various times. Your goal is to enact more of the behaviors from the "want to win" list and fewer from the "want to be perfect" list.

If you **want to win** (play well), here is what you should do:

1. Be focused on the present point
2. Maintain good body language regardless of what is happening around you
3. Be calm and use your breathing to keep your muscles relaxed
4. Give your best effort throughout and never stop competing
5. Encourage yourself to keep going
6. Strive to perform your best on every single point
7. Use routines to help you maintain focus
8. Always believe you can succeed
9. Be fair and respectful at all times
10. Be excited and grateful to compete
11. Understand that you don't have to win every point to win the match
12. Choose to be confident in your abilities
13. Look for opportunities to break your opponent mentally
14. Forgive yourself for mistakes and move on

If you **want to be perfect**, here is what you *will* do:

1. Get overly emotional when you win or lose a point, especially when you lose one

2. Keep your focus in the past on a mistake or lost opportunity
3. Not try as hard when you're down in a match
4. Let your body language, breathing and self-talk be dictated by everything going on around you – and it will all be negative
5. Make excuses for why you lost or played badly
6. Be broken mentally by your opponent
7. Act in a way that doesn't make you proud
8. Judge yourself after every point
9. Choose to have low confidence in yourself and your shots

I know that it may have been tough to read the behaviors on the "want to be perfect" list as we have all been there at some point, myself included, and will probably be there again in the future. However, with this new awareness, you can catch yourself in these behaviors and try to adjust them so that what you are doing on the court is helping you with the long-term mission of winning the match. If you play a sport other than tennis, the same concepts apply.

Behavior while competing isn't always going to be perfect either but strive to align your actions in competition with your desire to succeed. This perspective is what "playing to win" truly means and will make you a great competitor.

24. A 4 STEP FRAMEWORK FOR WINNING

Have you ever heard of the Marshmallow Test? If not, check it out on YouTube as it's quite humorous, but also informative. The object of the test is to gauge how well children can delay gratification in the presence of temptation. It has been shown that those who can delay gratification are typically more successful in life than others.

While playing in a social doubles event recently, it occurred to me that this concept plays out in sports as well. In my last match of the evening, I was paired up with a talented, but somewhat inconsistent player. Let's call him John. John loves hitting spectacular shots. If he has the choice between hitting a "boring" but correct shot up the middle, or a flashy winner that will clip the edge of the line, he'll pick the flashy shot 9 out of 10 times. And of those 9, he'll probably miss 5 (or more). By playing this way, John is constantly seeking the thrill of the winner with very little focus on the overall outcome of the match. His emotional swings from point to point show that he values this immediate gratification much more than winning. In fact, he told me that he detests "boring" tennis. Unfortunately for John, boring often wins, and winning in this context represents the delayed gratification that most competitors say they want.

When we step out onto the court or the field, our goal as competitors is to perform our best so that we can win. To be a great competitor, you must learn to make choices and decisions that support that goal. Reacting emotionally to plays or points shows that you don't have the big picture in mind and that you don't understand how these plays/points cumulatively add up to the desired result. Let's look at a basic framework for the proper focus required to give yourself the best chance of winning.

1. **Know the scoring system of your sport and the different types of situations that may arise.** For example, the scoring system in tennis is hierarchical. To win a match, you need to win sets. Sets are comprised of games, and games are comprised of points. At the end of a match, cumulative points and cumulative games are irrelevant, and it is possible to win more points than your opponent, but still lose the match. That means there are specific points and games that are more important than others. Many tennis players don't get that and therefore react angrily to losing points that are often inconsequential. In other sports, the scoring systems may be slightly simpler, but they all have unique situations. These situations call for specific approaches so that the team can score points appropriately. Know these situations and know what you should be doing in them so that your decision-making and choices are in support of playing your best and winning.

2. **Stay calm and rational.** Emotional reactions, both positive and negative, can cloud your judgement and are often a waste of energy. After a play or point is completed, simply reflect on its impact to the larger context of what you are trying to achieve. That will lead you to what do on the next play.

3. **Focus on the next play/point.** Most sports have natural breaks in action that allow you to reset yourself and get focused on the next play. Your goal during this in between play time is to be physically and mentally prepared to play your best on that next play. That means understanding the situation, having a plan in your head, and

being positive and optimistic about your abilities to succeed on that next play. What you do in between plays/points should be a routine that you go through every time.

4. **Repeat steps 2 and 3 over and over and over again until the contest is over.** Staying calm, having a high IQ in your sport, and focusing on what's important (the next play or point) is the formula for consistent and cumulative success throughout a game/match.

After my last set with John, we got to talking and I said to him that he might go to bed that evening dreaming of some of the spectacular winners that he hit, but I'll go to bed knowing that I won. Which would you prefer?

25. THREE THINGS TO DO TO BE A BETTER FIGHTER

When everything is going wrong in your performance, there is one facet of the mental game that can salvage the day: your fighting spirit. If you continue to fight for your best performance, even on your worst day, you still have a chance of succeeding in the end. The persistence and intensity that you bring to competition defines your fighting spirit, and the best competitors are full of fight.

Although we know that the brain does not operate in similar fashion to a computer, I believe a comparison will be useful to explain how mental toughness works. In order for your computer to function properly, its operating system relies on a number of inter-dependent processes that allow it to run software, monitor activity, allocate memory, save files, etc. Mental toughness is also comprised of processes that enable your mental game to function at a high level. These processes represent skills such as focus, confidence, motivation, self-control, intensity, fighting spirit, positivity, and decision-making. You may add others to this list. Depending on the relative strengths and weaknesses of your mental game, some of these processes may be dependent on others. For example, if your focus goes down, you may lose your ability to control your emotions (self-control). These dependent relationships differ among athletes. Other processes may be more independent and able to sustain themselves amidst breakdowns. The goal today is to help you make fighting spirit one of those processes that is independent and never goes off-line. It is a skill that can be strengthened.

To help you develop fighting spirit and turn it into a strength, I want to highlight three basic skills that need additional practice: motivation, focus, and best effort

Start With Why

To be a great fighter, you need a personally compelling reason as to why you compete. If you're not inspired to be your best in your sport, it becomes easy to quit in the heat of competition. Write the answers to the following questions to develop this compelling why:

- Why am I here (practice, event)?
- Why is this important to me?
- What is my ultimate goal?
- What is my perspective on excellence?
- What is success?

After answering these questions, do you have a more compelling reason to fight harder in your competitions? If not, discuss your answers with a coach or trusted person and get his/her perspective. Then write the answers to these questions again, and repeat that process until you feel motivated by your Why.

Perspective

In order to maintain your fighting spirit, you must understand what is truly important in competition and focus on that. There are so many distractions in sports: the last play, the consequences of winning and losing, what other people think. None of this matters if you want to perform your best. You have to learn to bring your full focus to the present.

THE MOST IMPORTANT POINT/PLAY/SHIFT IS
THE NEXT ONE!

If you're always focused on the present, you have a good perspective on what is important, and your fighting spirit will stay strong. To learn to be more present focused, try the following:

- Meditation
- Use a "Reset Button" while you compete – forget the last play and move on to the next.
- Ask yourself, "What am I going to do right now?"

Your ability to fight in competition can be depleted by focusing on distractions. Know what is important to your best performance (perspective) and focus on that. Your fighting spirit will be strong.

Practice Your Best Effort

Most athletes report trying harder in competition than they do in practice, and that sounds natural. Unfortunately, that means you are probably only able to give 80 to 90% of your total energy capacity in competition because you've never really practiced best effort as a skill. Change that; push the limits of your energy capacity and see your fighting spirit soar.

- Try harder and harder in practice
- Never give up on a play or point
- Push yourself to the point of muscle failure
- Set process goals for your practices and use best effort to reach them

Training your best effort as a skill in practice will ensure that you will have the energy you need to keep up your fighting spirit throughout your competition. One of my favorite quotes from *The Fighter's Mind* by Sam Sheridan on this topic is "…it's a battle of will, and nothing breaks will like fatigue." Fatigue takes your fighting spirit offline, and that is exactly what you do not want to happen. Start increasing the limits of your best effort today.

If you are able to make improvements in your motivation, focus, and best effort, you will become a great fighter, and you will see improvements in your competitive performances. Give it a go!

26. DON'T GET ANGRY WHEN YOU COMPETE

As a young tennis player, I had a bad temper. I didn't like making mistakes. I didn't like losing points. The root of my anger wasn't a lack of emotional control, but rather because my thoughts were fixated on those mistakes and lost points, and that frustrated me greatly. If only I could be perfect on the court!

Once I learned to adjust my focus to what mattered at that moment, my angry outbursts stopped, and the quality of my performances improved. It is through my own experience with such behavior that I want to give you 4 reasons why you should never get angry when you compete.

1. You're giving away information to your opponent

When you get angry and show it, you are telling your opponents that whatever they are doing, it's working. It's a clear sign you are starting to break down mentally and the entire world can see it. How you react to adversity during competition is the most visible sign of your mental toughness, and displays of anger are a sign of mental weakness. Do you really want to be giving away that information? It's the opposite of having a poker face. Can you imagine professional poker players reacting in anger when they are dealt a bad hand? Their professional careers would be short. Be mindful of the information that your body language and audible self-talk convey to your opponent. Your opponent should only see what you want them to see.

2. You're not focused on what matters

The last play, point or shift no longer matter. It's in the past and is beyond your control. Thinking about it won't change the result, but it will serve to upset you further and it will take your focus away from your performance. Whatever you're doing right now is most important, and this moment requires your full attention if you are to succeed in the long term. When I realized this, my bad temper disappeared.

3. You make bad decisions

Do you know anyone who makes good decisions in life when they're angry? I doubt it. You're simply too emotional in the moment, and the body chemistry of anger corrupts your ability to make good decisions as well as your motor skills, neither of which is good for an athlete. Quite simply, anger is a waste of energy. On the other hand, positive emotions help decision-making and creativity.

4. You DON'T play better when you get angry

Every now and then, an athlete will tell me that he plays better when he gets angry. Sometimes the athletes who say this confuse anger with intensity. Those terms are not the same, and I would agree that increased intensity, to a certain point, can lead to better performance. However, the idea that anger leads to better performance is a myth. It is a story you tell yourself to rationalize your own behavior. When you tell yourself this story, you are confusing causality with correlation. To understand this better, let's consider the concept of "regression to the mean." The premise is that we all have an average level of play. When we are playing below our average for an extended period of time, anger can ensue at some point. Consider this situation from the perspective of probability. Are you more likely to continue to play below your average level and possibly worse, or are you more likely to play better and come back to your average level? The answer is that you are more likely to play better and come back to your average level of play. The cause of your improvement in performance is purely statistical, not your angry reaction. The anger just happens to occur at that low point in your performance, so you associate it with the improvement in play. If you truly believe that you play better when you get angry, then why don't you keep getting angry even after your performance has improved? For a more complete explanation of this, read Daniel Kahneman's book *Thinking Fast and Slow*.

If you're an emotional competitor, I'd like you to keep these 4 points in mind during your next competition. Try to pinpoint the root cause of your anger and frustration so that you can determine some strategies to deal with it. You will be a better competitor in the long-term if you channel your energy, and your anger, in more productive ways.

27. WHAT TO DO WHEN YOU'RE NOT PLAYING WELL

A short story from a practice match I played recently...

The wind was in my face and I was getting ready to serve for the first time in the match. I don't have a very big serve and even a little bit of wind against me can make it more ordinary than usual. My opponent was an aggressive returner who often liked to follow his shots into the net, and while I don't mind that so much, I'm typically looking to grind out points from the baseline. That's my comfort zone. Based on those factors, I was feeling some pressure to do "something" with my first serve. Naturally, the first one went straight into the net. Uh oh.

But hold on a second. After that first serve went into the net, I became very aware of what went wrong. I rushed through my entire service ritual and motion, starting with bouncing the ball way too fast. That rushing led to my toss being too low and too far in front. My muscles were tense, and the entire service motion was anything but fluid. How could I possibly expect my serve to go in with all of this going on?

This realization took about 1 second and it helped me make the adjustments I needed. I took a deep breath and lowered my shoulders on the exhale. I bounced up and down, and shook the tension out of my right arm. In my service ritual, I bounced the ball slowly, and stayed slow and smooth throughout the entire motion. I didn't care if my opponent was coming into the net or not. The result was that I served well for the rest of the match.

In working with students on their mental game, this is a story that I rarely hear. Based on the first paragraph above, the usual story would be "I didn't serve well today." And that story leads to a loss of confidence and a poor performance. If adjustments were made, they were all technical in nature and didn't result in much improvement. There was no awareness of body and mind.

Through practices such as yoga, meditation, and rhythmic breathing, I have become much better at being aware of how I feel when I compete. My mind and body communicate much better than in the past. This is important because regardless of your sport, if you are making mistakes, it's most likely due to tension in your muscles which is leading to mechanical breakdowns and rushing. To start playing well, you need to be aware of how you are feeling and know what to do about it.

Many students ask me "what should I do when I'm not playing well?" It's a great question and it is the right question. We have to DO something. My answer to this question normally begins with "Well, you're not going to like my answer..." And I start off with that because I know most players don't want to focus on doing the activities that I mentioned in the story above. They don't believe that breathing, body language, and body awareness are important factors to performing well. They feel that everything is about technique. However, being aware of your body and mind is critical and that's where you must start.

To play well, you must feel well. Your body and mind must be in harmony. When you are not playing well, all of your actions and adjustments should be about changing how you feel. From there, your technique will improve. Here's a quick list of things to do:

- Take deep and rhythmic breaths
- Lower your shoulders on the exhale

- Bounce up and down, and shake out your arms and legs
- Walk with confidence and determination - shoulders back, positive energy, a bit of swagger
- Take more time between points (for other sports, look to slow the pace of the game down)
- Slow down your mechanics with an aim to be smooth - that doesn't mean decelerate through the motion; just go slow so you can establish a rhythm
- Loosen the grip on your racquet (or stick, ball, etc.) - a lot of tension begins with how tightly we hold the racquet
- Be patient with the process of making yourself feel better

If you do the above consistently in your performance, you'll start to feel more in control of yourself and your body and mind will be in harmony. After you have achieved a state of feeling better, it will be easier to make more complex adjustments if they are needed. Your mind will also be better prepared to handle whatever pressures may have been contributing to the tension you were feeling.

I recommend that you write the items above on a piece of paper and bring it onto the court with you. Read it before you play and on change-overs. Use this checklist from the start of the match and you probably will not have to ask the question, "what do I do when I'm not playing well?"

28. STRATEGIES FOR THE PLAYER WHO GETS TIGHT

Have you ever felt tight or tense while competing? If you're like most people, myself included, you have probably felt this way at some point in your competitive career. Sometimes it just happens under pressure and at other times, that tight and tense feeling is present from the beginning. Whatever the situation, it doesn't feel good, and that tightness in our muscles prevents our best game from emerging.

This topic comes up a lot with my students and it's something I need to improve on myself. Tight and tense muscles can be a huge energy drain, and for us tennis players, we tend to hit the ball short in the court with limited power. We often play more conservatively and make errors into the net. Instead, we would like to look like Roger Federer who appears loose, relaxed and floating around the court. Roger always has confidence in his shots, and we need to do the same to be successful.

What can we do about this? Here are a few points to consider in your competitive training.

1. Treat Relaxation as a Skill

We all know that we perform better when our muscles are loose, but we don't all know how to reduce muscle tension at a given moment. We may not have that kind of awareness with our bodies, and therefore it's necessary to view relaxation skills and exercises as an important part of your competitive skills training.

2. Train Relaxation off the Court

Like any skill, learning to relax and reduce muscle tension requires practice and patience. This article on Relaxation Techniques (http://www.helpguide.org/articles/stress/relaxation-techniques-for-stress-relief.htm) has some excellent suggestions for ways to practice and improve, and I especially like Progressive Relaxation as a technique because it helps you build awareness and communication with your muscles. Jeff Greenwald mentions this same technique in his book *The Best Tennis of Your Life* (Chapter 43) so that is another resource for your training. Additionally, consider adding some of the breathing exercises described in the article linked above. The topic of the article is "stress relief", however that's not what we are trying to do. We aren't relieving stress; we are training a productive reaction to stress that will allow us to handle it better.

Commit to practicing these techniques several days a week. As you do them, associate some "cue words" with these activities so that you can use these words on the court when you need them. For example, while you're doing progressive relaxation, think "loose muscles." You can then use "loose muscles" as a phrase to initiate your relaxation response while you're playing.

3. Train Relaxation on the Court

When feeling tight on the court, there are several things you can do.

1. **Focus on your breath between points** - use rhythmic breathing (consistent inhales and exhales)

to slow your heart rate and clear your mind. This breathing technique will naturally relax you.

2. **Bounce up and down, and shake the tension out of your arms** - do this before the start of every point. Doing it once or twice won't have the desired effect. It needs to be done consistently for a sustained period of time.

3. **Use your cue words** - as you are doing the above 2 techniques, repeat your cue words in your mind ("loose muscles"). This will help you to trigger the relaxation response you've been training off court.

4. **Progressive relaxation on change of sides** - when you sit down for the change over, do some progressive relaxation for your hands, arms, and shoulders.

4. Keep a Training Log

Since relaxation and tension reduction are skills, you're not necessarily going to be great at them right away. Use a training log to evaluate and monitor how you feel on and off the court. After a few weeks, compare how you feel today with how you felt during week 1 of your training. You should notice that you are getting better at inducing the relaxation response and that how you are playing in competition feels better.

You may be thinking that training the relaxation response is a bit out there or over the top, but I believe that this is one of those "little things" that will add up to better performances on the court. Try the above for several weeks and see if you notice a difference (via your training log). These techniques don't take huge amounts of time, and they will have a cumulative effect.

29. THE 5 PARTS OF YOUR COMPETITIVE SELF

All great competitors have a keen sense of what their body state should be during competition so that they perform at their top level. This means that they are in touch with how their muscles feel, what they're thinking, what they're feeling, etc. Their body state is their body chemistry. Competitive situations alter body chemistry, and it's critical to understand some of the levers that you can use to get yourself in the right state.

There are 5 parts to what I call the "Competitive Self" that can help you manage and adjust your body state so that you're performing at an optimal level under pressure. These 5 parts are inter-dependent and have some overlap, but are also independent enough to be monitored separately.

1. **Your Breathing** - The rhythm and depth of your breath are key components of controlling your body chemistry. Rhythmic breathing can enable your mind to reach a state of coherence that will allow it to focus better in the face of competition. Deep breaths are not necessarily important on their own, but shallow breaths can make you more nervous and tense. Use your breath to help you relax and lower your heart rate.

2. **Your Body Language** - What image are you reflecting to your opponent and yourself? Make sure that it's a confident and strong image that shows you're going to be fighting till the end. There should

be no sign of weakness or negativity. Body language is a strong influencer on the other 5 parts in this formula.

3. **Your Self-Talk** - Keep your self-talk brief and focused on what you need to do. When you're in the zone, the mind is generally quiet, so a lot of self-talk can be detrimental to performance because you might be over-thinking. The tone of your self-talk should be positive, encouraging, supportive and confident.

4. **Your Emotional State** - While there is some literature that states that anger can lead to performing better, it's a tough emotion to control in that way. I think of it like riding a bucking bronco that you have to steer in a particular direction. It's easier said than done. Alternatively, your emotional state should be predominantly positive and unwaveringly optimistic. You should feel excited about competing and enjoying the challenge.

5. **Your Focus** - Learn to narrow your focus down to the only parts of your performance that matter. That means being in the moment and focusing on the very next point, play, shift, shot, etc. Focusing on anything broader than that opens you up to distractions or things that don't actually matter to your performance.

Being mentally tough and a great competitor is all about making the decisions that keep these 5 parts of your Competitive Self aligned with the mission of performing your best and winning. While getting angry may feel like the proper natural reaction given what we sometimes see on television, it is in my opinion a sign of mental weakness. It disrupts the optimal aspects of the 5 parts, most especially Focus. When you get angry, you're focused on the past and no matter how much you think about the past, it isn't going to change. This is a lesson that many coaches need to learn not only for themselves, but for the effect that their anger has on their players. That kind of anger isn't a sign of how tough you are. It actually shows how little control you have over your own emotions and what a poor understanding you have of mental toughness.

In order to perform your best, monitor and be accountable for the 5 parts of Your Competitive Self. Remind yourself of these things before you practice/compete and then evaluate yourself afterward so you can learn from how you did.

30. HOW TO SUCCEED IN CRITICAL MOMENTS

There are moments or situations in all sports that are crucial to deciding the outcome. In tennis, it might be a tie-breaker or a 10-point tie-breaker in lieu of a 3rd set. In football, it's the two-minute drill. Every sport has at least one, and to be the best competitor you can be, you need to recognize the importance of these moments because they are both exciting and dangerous when it comes to the result.

Over the years, I have worked with many competitors who struggle at these times in games and matches. They're good enough to get themselves to the critical moment, but they lack the necessary competitive skills to consistently succeed in these situations against equal or greater opposition. Let's look at a few typical responses to reaching these critical moments.

Contentment/Satisfaction

When facing opposition that you believe to be "better" than you are, you can become contented that you have pushed the opposition to a certain competitive point. For example, in tennis you may observe this when a player takes the opponent to 4-all in a set, and then begins thinking to himself that he's quite happy that he's won 4 games in a set. Unfortunately, this feeling of satisfaction is deadly when it comes to winning because you're already happy prior to the conclusion. The motivation to keep competing at your top level is now gone. Invariably, the better player will win this set 6-4 because he isn't concerned with winning 4 games, he's concerned with winning 6.

Dread

The game is on the line and the spotlight is now on you. How do you react? If you're like a lot of athletes, you don't want to be in that situation. You don't want to be the person who let the team down when it really mattered or the one who choked when the pressure was on. Even if you're a great competitor now, you've been here. You've experienced it because it's part of the learning process albeit a painful one. I remember playing in a Little League All Star Game when I was 12. It was the bottom of the 6th and we were trailing 6-5. There were 2 outs and I was in the on-deck circle. My thoughts at that moment? I wanted the player at bat to make the 3rd out. I didn't want to be the one who lost the game especially since I had made an error in the top of the inning that allowed the go-ahead run for our opponents. This was not the attitude of a great competitor, but it is a common one.

Lack of Recognition

The last typical reaction to the important moments in competition is actually no reaction or recognition at all. It's a lack of understanding that something big is about to happen and you need to pay attention. If you're competing against an opponent with a lot of experience, she's going to step up her focus and intensity at this moment in time. If you don't do the same, you'll probably lose because you didn't realize something extra was required. I see and hear this reaction all the time and it can be a difficult hurdle to conquer for young competitors.

What Should You Do? 4 Steps

1. **Do you know the critical moments in your sport?** You have to know what these are if you're going to succeed at them. As mentioned earlier, each sport has some typical situations so talk to your coach if you're unsure of what they are. Discuss ways of recognizing them when they occur.

2. **Love these moments!** It's in the critical moments that we separate ourselves as competitors from the rest of the crowd. You have to relish the opportunity you have in front of you. Even if you typically dread these moments, you must say "I love the two-minute drill" or "I love tie-breakers". While you may be lying to yourself at first, repeating these affirmations will seep into your mind and help you reframe your attitude. Soon you'll be much more positive and optimistic when the time comes.

3. **Raise your focus level and intensity.** Getting to this moment isn't what should be satisfying us. Succeeding in this moment is our new motivation and since the result is still in doubt, we must bring more energy and intensity to the situation. From a mental perspective, we must "go for it!" Since optimal excitement and arousal levels differ for all competitors, this will take some trial and error on your part, but don't give up. Once you find your optimal level of energy and intensity in these moments, your success rate will improve dramatically.

4. **Play your game and simply execute.** Just because we are raising our awareness, focus, energy and intensity, that doesn't mean we should all of a sudden change our game plan. Playing your game is what got you to this point so don't abandon it now in favor of something that you're not quite as good at executing. There may be times when you take a bit

more risk, but it should only be within the framework of what you are good at (aka, Your Competitive Identity).

Work on these 4 steps in practice and competition. It will take some experimentation on your part, but that's how we learn and improve. Through patience and hard work, you'll start winning in these critical moments.

31. USE A POSITIVE PHYSICAL RESPONSE TO FOCUS

It's no secret that you need excellent focus to be a great competitor. The best athletes in the world do this well and while they may make it look easy, it isn't easy to do for long periods of time. There are a lot of things going on that are competing for your attention, and most of these have nothing to do with you playing your best in this moment. To perform at your peak, you have to be fully focused on what you can control.

In my work with tennis players, I help them incorporate a specific positive physical response into what they do immediately after a point is over. It's simple, easy to do, and very quick. If you were watching some random points of these players, you might not even notice it. And while we are talking about tennis in this chapter, the reasons for why we do this are the same for sports such as golf, volleyball, football, baseball/softball, etc.

Here is the physical response I've been asking players to use: Once a point is over, place the racquet into your non-dominant hand and hold it at the throat. Place the thumb of your dominant hand at the bottom of the string-bed or on your vibration dampener, and press it.

That's it. As I said, it's very simple and here are 3 reasons you should incorporate this into your game.

1. You need a Reset Button

Great focus and great performance in tennis requires that you ALWAYS have a "next point" mentality. By moving on from the last point, you are now able to more clearly focus on what you need to do on the next point. This is the "Reset Button" concept at work. Programming an immediate physical response after a point is over is helpful in taking away that moment in which you normally judge yourself based on the last point so that you can move on to the next point. Forget what just happened; strive to perform your best on the next one.

2. Physical Response is More Effective

When I first started utilizing this Reset Button concept many years ago, I didn't have a physical response or ritual. I tried to use my self-talk to remind me to reset, and while this was somewhat effective, I found that completing a physical ritual immediately after a point was far more effective. For me, the vibration dampener became my physical Reset Button and my ability to remember to do this improved. Press your vibration dampener or strings to reset your focus, and at the same time tell yourself to "reset".

3. Project a Confident and Calm Image

This positive physical response is a very simple 2-step process, and even though it is simple and quick, it's amazing how good it looks on video. During training sessions, we video the players doing this and then watch it with them. I ask them for their description of what they are seeing in themselves. Confident and calm are the most popular responses. They like how it looks. They like how it helps them take a bit more time and move on from the last point.

Confident and calm is the image we want to be projecting after every point, first for ourselves and second for our opponent. By projecting this confident and calm image on a consistent basis, you are showing your opponent that you are unbreakable today.

If you are a tennis player, try the positive physical response I have described above and incorporate the Reset Button into your game. If you play another sport, design a simple positive physical response that will work for you. Adopt a next point/play/shot/pitch mentality into your performance, and your ability to focus and perform well will dramatically improve.

32. DEVELOP A QUIET MIND

There are certain thoughts, emotions and physical indicators that are common to being in the "zone." Examples are complete focus, low anxiety, high confidence, energetic, fun, and the feeling of being in complete control. When I work with groups or teams on defining these characteristics of the zone, usually one person in the audience will mention a specific item that I think is tremendously important, but often overlooked: a quiet mind.

What do I mean by a quiet mind? When we are performing our best, everything we do feels automatic. Our body is executing flawlessly, and our minds aren't getting in the way with a lot of extraneous thoughts. In fact, our mind is working efficiently. The messages in our self-talk are simple and motivational. There's no high-level strategic thinking going on because it's not needed. The mind is essentially "quiet".

This characteristic of the zone has actually been proven in scientific work. An article in *New Scientist* magazine described how soldiers being trained for military combat were connected to a battery with electrodes on the forearm and at the temple to induce a state in which a test subject could learn a skill faster by passing an electrical current through the brain. Not only did the soldiers learn their skills faster (up to 2.5 times faster), but as a result of this, the test subjects went into the zone, and scientists noticed that the amount of activity in the frontal lobe of the neocortex was minimal. The frontal lobe is the part of our brains that separates us from the rest of the animal kingdom. It is where all of our complex thinking activities occur and since this area was "quiet" we know that the individual being trained with the electrical current wasn't using higher level thinking. He was simply letting his body do the activity.

As competitors, we are often not in the zone. So how does knowing that a quiet mind is part of the zone help us get there when we are struggling? Think about keeping your self-talk simple and productive so that you can begin to reduce the complex and often unproductive thoughts going through your head. Emotions and frustration will also engage the thought processes in your frontal lobe and will take you away from where you want to go. Relax and take deep breaths. Focus on your breath. Let your body do what it has been trained to do. If you trust your abilities, you'll be able to do this more easily than the competitor who's struggling with confidence. Relaxing your body will relax your mind. If you can master the skill of connecting your mind and body, you'll find yourself in the zone more and more often when you're competing under pressure. That's where we want to be and that's mental toughness.

33. HOW TO CHANGE YOUR BODY LANGUAGE

Want a quick pick-me-up while you're competing? Pay attention to your body language and make sure it's positive, strong, confident, determined, and shows that you're willing to fight. The connection between our minds and bodies is very strong, and negative behavior in one area almost always results in negativity in the other. The good news is that this also works on the positive side of the equation, and changing your body language is often less challenging than altering or stopping your thoughts.

Athletes who display negative body language in competition don't realize how much information they're giving away to their opponents. There's a reason you need a "poker face" in poker, as you don't want to give away your strategy at the card table. Competitive athletes should learn to adopt that same philosophy so that their opponents can't read what's going on in their head via their body language. If an athlete is displaying negative body language, here's what he/she is telling the world:

- My opponent's game is bothering me
- I can't handle adversity
- I can't control my emotions
- I've lost focus on what is important
- I'm not mentally tough
- I am breaking down mentally

All of these signs give the opponent more confidence to continue their strategy because they know it's working. The athlete with negative body language ultimately defeats himself through self-sabotage.

How do you deal with this when it comes up in competition? Use a little trick called "if, then". This is essentially a mental planning trick. If a particular situation might occur, then you want to have a pre-programmed response for it. For example, *if* I get negative in competition, *then* I'm going to walk with confidence and purpose, and display a strong image. If you plan this out before you compete, you're more likely to be able to turn around a negative situation than with no planning whatsoever.

The next time you go out to compete, do some "if, then" planning and show the world through your body language that you're a great competitor. You'll be amazed at the impact of such a simple change.

34. RESPECT MAKES YOU BETTER

A few years ago, I was playing in a league tennis match and was paired against a player who had a reputation for on-court shenanigans and creating controversy. When I realized who I was playing, I had a decision to make. What should my approach to this player be? Conventional wisdom tells us to be on-guard for the slightest indiscretion or infraction with this type of opponent and not to back down if there's a confrontation. Our reptilian brain, the one that identifies threats and spurs us into action, takes over to help us deal with the difficult player. Now, if this were the 1990's when I was a weaker competitor, that's exactly the approach I would have taken.

However, if I think back to those days when I opted for that approach, it didn't help me play my best tennis. It took the focus off of my own performance and if anything, was a major distraction. If something questionable did occur in the match, my immediate reaction was confrontational, and that escalated the situation and made it worse. I'm sure that my own body language and demeanor were so obviously negative that my opponent picked up on it thus making him more defensive right from the start of the match.

What's a competitor to do in this situation when he wants to play well and win? What did I decide to do? In this match, I went against conventional wisdom and decided to be ultra-respectful and polite to my opponent. If he hit a good shot, I would compliment him on it. I would say thank you whenever he hit the tennis balls to my side of the court. I would remain calm and display positive body language at all times. I would not show him up by saying "C'mon!" in a loud voice. And guess what? It totally worked. Not only did we not have a single issue, I got him saying "nice shot" and "thank you" to me! Chalk up a victory for attracting the kind of behavior you want out of someone else by behaving that way yourself.

One of the character traits that I monitor in my own performances in practice and competition is **Respect**: respect for my opponent, respect for the game, respect for my teammates, etc. When I behave this way, I know it makes me feel better and it makes me more positive. I play better, and I stay focused on the right behaviors. I can take pride in how I handle myself in a competitive environment. Having respect for your opponent in competition is important because that person is making you better. They are giving you something to measure yourself against and you should be grateful and thankful for that opportunity. Every competitor deserves respect because it takes courage to put yourself on the line and compete in a public forum. So many people avoid competitive situations and therefore it's important to note how courageous and gutsy it is to go out there and try to play your best under pressure.

The next time you're in a difficult situation with an opponent, consider approaching it from a position of respect. I can't guarantee that it will work every time for you like it worked for me in this match, but I can guarantee that you'll be proud of your own behavior in a competitive situation. That builds character.

35. CREATING MAXIMUM ENERGY

Life is about energy management as we alternate between expending energy and recovering energy. The goal is to bring the maximum amount of energy possible to everything you do so that you can perform at your peak. To do this, you need to know how to increase your energy reserves as well as rest and recharge when necessary. Many people feel that energy management is a function of time management and because of that, there never seems to be enough time to do what's needed to get in shape, be healthy, eat well, feel rested, etc. If you reverse the relationship and make time management a function of energy management, then maximum energy is the priority and your calendar becomes a means of supporting that belief.

So how does this work? If maximum energy is your priority, here are some of the things that should be in your calendar:

- Consistent sleep habits: going to bed and waking up at the same times, minimum 8 hours per night
- Workouts
- Practice
- Recovery/Relaxation
- Breakfast, Lunch and Dinner (with planned meals)
- Snack time
- Reading
- Connecting with friends and family
- Journaling / Goal Setting / Planning for the day/week
- Meditation / Visualization / Mindfulness activities

I'm sure you can think of more. The point is to use your daily/weekly calendar as a tool to maximize your energy rather than letting your calendar drive you into the ground. Each of the items above needs to be viewed as an appointment that cannot be canceled. They are non-negotiable blocks of time dedicated to helping you maximize your energy. Still think you don't have time? I challenge you to look at the time you may be spending watching television, playing video games, using social media sites, etc. Cutting back on just one hour of those activities per week can make a huge difference in improving your energy.

Why do all of this? The amount of physical energy you have drives the quality of your life. When you increase your energy, you'll be more motivated. You'll be more focused. And you'll be more positive and optimistic. All of those things are ingredients for being a great competitor in sports and in life. Even if you think you're already good at this stuff, you can always be better. Take your energy to new levels and your performances will follow.

36. WHAT TO DO AGAINST A SUPERIOR OPPONENT

There are times in competition in which we face opponents who are better than we are. They may have a better record than us or perhaps they have more achievements. Regardless, that's not nearly as important as how we react to the challenge of facing this opponent. In this type of matchup, our mental attitude and approach is critical in determining if we'll be competitive or not. Let's review some less than optimal mindsets when facing a superior opponent. Some of them are clearly related and intertwined.

Over-Respect

When we over-respect opponents, we put them on a pedestal that makes them seem unbeatable. They are no longer human, but are instead invincible opponents with few flaws, if any. This attitude basically leads to losing the competition in the locker room. The result has been decided before the event has even begun.

Lack of Effort

"If we're playing somebody who's better than we are, what's the point of even trying, right? They're better than we are and they're going to win anyway."

Obviously, this attitude is not that of a great competitor and it represents one of the most basic emotional responses to competition - quitting. Your opponent will love this attitude as they'll barely have to sweat to win.

Contentment/Satisfaction

As I mentioned in a previous chapter on Succeeding in the Critical Moments, we can often become satisfied with ourselves once we've pushed our superior opponent to a certain point in the competition. We've made them work a little bit and perhaps we've done better than we thought, and now we can lose without shame. Our effort and focus at the end of the event will wane and the superior player will emerge victorious. Others will know via the score that we were competitive and our self-esteem is intact.

What Should Our Mental Approach Be?

1. Respect everyone, fear no one. My friend and coach, Steve Host, said this to a group of junior tennis players a few years ago, and while he may not have coined the phrase, it is right on in terms of the competitive mindset. Superior physical skills do not necessarily mean superior competitive skills. You have to bring a 100% fighting spirit to every event you play. Don't lose before you've even begun.

2. We are all human. None of us are perfect and that includes our supposedly superior opponent. We all have bad days and we all make mistakes. This might be the day that our opponent isn't feeling his or her best.

3. Make Your Opponent Work Hard. One of my mantras when I play a tennis tournament is that no matter who I play, I want them to remember me because I made them work hard. I may lose the match, and I certainly lose plenty of matches, but the match will have taken a physical toll on my opponent. Make it your goal to let no team or opponent ever forget how hard you made them work. You may be rewarded for that the next time you face them.

4. Not all great players are great competitors. There are many teams and athletes who are great front-runners. They are used to dominating opponents and blowing them out on the scoreboard. Because of this, they may not be quite so confident when the event gets close and the pressure is on. Do your best to keep the score close and you may be surprised at how the supposedly superior opponent reacts under pressure. At the very least, expose them to as much pressure as you can and keep working hard. Don't be satisfied and let them off the hook. Make them prove that they can succeed. It's possible that they may choke.

In situations when you are facing a superior opponent, what is your typical reaction? Write it down and see if there is any faulty logic that matches the typical reactions I mentioned above. Next, write down what you want your approach to be in the future when you face better opponents. You need to prepare for this because it will happen. Discuss it with your coach and incorporate this new approach into your training. This situation is a clear example of when competitive skills can trump physical ones.

37. HOW TO IMPRESS YOUR COACH

If you are a high school or college athlete, you know what it is like to go through try-outs and practices in the pre-season. It can be a nerve-wracking time. There may be uncertainty as to whether you'll play or where you might be in the lineup, and your fate isn't always in your hands. You can perform your best in practice, but the final decision is often up to your coach or coaches, and you may not know what they are watching. How do you feel about that?

Many athletes have no issue with this situation whatsoever. They perform their best in practice and they're confident enough in themselves that they simply expect the coach to make the right decision. Usually the superstars of the team or the top players have this attitude. It's helped them get to where they are.

But others may feel differently when playing in front of coaches, including some superstars. The perceived lack of control over the decision of will they play, or where will they play, can cause anxiety. The buildup to practicing in front of the coach becomes an event in itself because we feel like we have to impress them. We may even look at our coaches as mythical and unapproachable figures who are intimidating to talk to. However, the reality is often quite different.

If you find yourself having some anxiety with trying to impress your coaches, here are some suggestions:

1. Don't impress, express yourself - You can't control the thoughts of other people and that's what you're trying to do when you focus on impressing your coaches. Instead, focus on being yourself in your performance. If you have a good sense of your identity as a competitor, then focus on that and what you do best (your strengths). If you can do that successfully and consistently, your coaches will be impressed.

2. Talk to your coaches - The vast majority of coaches love interacting with their athletes, but because of the size of teams, it can be difficult to strengthen any one relationship. That's where you come in. Regardless of your relationship with your coach, commit to taking that relationship to another level. Let him/her know how much you want to improve, how much you care about the team, how you want to contribute more to the team, how you would like to display more leadership and ownership of what happens over the course of the season. Your coach will love this! The more effort a coach sees you putting into the team, the more effort that coach will put into you. In the process, you'll humanize your coach and won't see him/her as unapproachable. Your coach will also be more likely to give you the benefit of the doubt when you have a poor performance because he/she knows how much you care.

3. Bring a positive character trait to practice/competition everyday - Is there something you're really good at from a character perspective? Loyalty, respect, integrity, humor, kindness, generosity, best effort, focus, etc.? Figure out a trait that is very important to you as a person and competitor, and commit to bringing that trait to practice and competition every day. Lead by example for your teammates and coaches. Whenever we bring our best selves to a situation, we have an excellent chance of flourishing. Now that will be impressive!

These 3 points are all things that you can control. Focus on what you can control and let that process do the impressing for you.

38. DEVELOP A MINDSET TO DEAL WITH NOISE

Ever find yourself wishing that someone would just be quiet while you're performing? I'm often asked about how tennis players can deal more effectively with crowds or an unruly spectator so that performance is not affected in a negative way. In most sports, crowd noise tends to be less of a distraction because it is the norm. It's expected. However, in sports such as golf and tennis, it's not the norm. Silence is. A tennis player's mental model of playing the sport doesn't include noise or heckling so when it occurs, distraction ensues, and performance typically degrades. High school tennis and college tennis can be challenges to a player's mental model on noise if he/she has only played tournament tennis to that point.

To improve performance in the presence of crowd noise, you must change your mental model of what is included in a normal tennis match. In other words, when you go on the court, you must expect and be prepared for crowd noise and heckling. When it occurs, accept it as normal and expected, and bring your focus back to your performance. It's unacceptable to blame your bad performance on crowd noise and then do nothing to be prepared for it the next time. If it bothers you the next time, don't blame the crowd. It's your fault for not being prepared. Mentally tough competitors don't make excuses; they make adjustments.

To aid in your preparation, you should develop what I call a Mindset Plan. To help you perform well in this situation, write down what you want the following dimensions to be when this occurs: your focus, your emotions, and a phrase or two that describes your attitude. If you can trigger these three dimensions of your mental game when crowd noise occurs, you'll be able to shift your focus back to your game more quickly and not let the crowd bother you.

As a competitor, it is your job to be prepared and to have a pre-programmed response to the distraction. Crowd noise and heckling ARE a part of the sport of tennis so be ready for it. Have a plan! You must understand that and focus on what makes you a great competitor.

39. DO YOU KNOW HOW TO PLAY BADLY WELL?

"The worse you're performing, the more you must work mentally and emotionally. The greatest and toughest art in golf is playing badly well. All the true greats have been masters at it."
-- JACK NICKLAUS

I love this quote from all-time golf great, Jack Nicklaus. When I read the phrase "playing badly well", I immediately think, "yes, yes, that's the difference between the greats and everyone else!" Let's unpack this bit of wisdom so that we can understand it more deeply and learn how to play badly well in competition and in life.

Every athlete has a physical game or abilities that are easily observed. We can see their technical skill, their speed, their strength, etc. However, it is much more difficult to measure the strength of an athlete's mental and emotional game especially before a competition has begun. For this reason, I like to think of every athlete as having an inner fortress of mental toughness representing their mental/emotional game. You can imagine it standing on the side of the field/court/etc. The Stoic philosophers of Ancient Greece and Rome referred to this fortress concept as the "inner citadel."

Throughout a competition, you must protect your fortress. You don't want to weaken your own fortress and you certainly don't want to allow your opponent (if you have one) to do so either. How you react and what you focus on while competing either weakens your fortress or strengthens it.

The fortress of mental toughness concept is critical to understanding how to play badly well. There must be a foundation of your fortress that never collapses. It must always remain in place and it cannot be compromised by any outside adversity. Weak to average competitors allow their fortresses to be smashed completely with pieces strewn all over the field or court.

That strong foundation is built on certain core beliefs and behaviors:

- Unshakable desire and determination to reach your objective
- High Effort and Energy level
- Focused Intensity
- Ability to take action and always move forward
- Unshakable Self-belief
- Persistence

You may be able to think of others, but I believe this is a good start. No matter what adversity you are facing in competition or in life, you cannot allow it to take these behaviors off-line. They are the foundation. Without them, you will give in to your negative emotions and defeat yourself. Unfortunately, this is what we see all too often even at the Division 1 collegiate level.

In conclusion, work on your foundation on and off the field of play so that the next time you are playing badly (there will be a next time!), you can do it better than in the past. Perhaps in the future, you will become one of the greats to whom Jack Nicklaus was referring.

40. MORE ADVICE FOR THE YOUNG COMPETITOR

I watch a lot of junior and college tennis, and I'm always paying attention to the competitiveness of players. The 10 points below are some general observations that I have made over the years while watching my students and their opponents compete. Each of the 10 items below are lessons that you can apply to your own performances regardless of sport.

1. Don't lose the match before you start

What you're thinking, what you're feeling and what you're doing before a match begins has a tremendous impact on how you will play. I recall a tournament a few years ago when I was watching various players around the tournament desk. The opponent of one of my students caught my eye and I could tell she wasn't ready. Her body language was low energy and she was arguing with her parents. It was obvious that she wasn't excited to compete. I knew this match was over before it began which was unfortunate for her because it was a winnable match. To compete at your best, use powerful body language to promote confidence and calmness so that you will be in a positive frame of mind when you arrive on court.

2. All styles of tennis are "real tennis"

I'm sure you have heard people refer to certain styles of play as not being "real tennis." Usually, this refers to a style that a player (or a parent) does not like facing such as pushing or moon-balls. These styles are not pretty or entertaining to watch as they require a great deal of patience and are used to frustrate opponents. However, I believe that these strategies are legitimate ways of competing. The objective for players is not to entertain others or to look good on the court; it is to break the opponent mentally in pursuit of winning the match. That's what your strategy and style should be focused on rather than simply playing in a manner that you think is correct. Thinking that your opponent's style of play is not "real tennis" will only distract you from what you need to do.

3. Don't leave your strengths on the sidelines

Sometimes when we play, we make bad choices about particular shots or strategies and these choices can lead to us not using our competitive strengths. When we don't use our strengths, we are not bringing our best performance that day. For example, I remember seeing one player in a tournament who has a heavy forehand that can draw errors opting for a flatter ball that ended up in the opponent's strike zone, while another player was being super aggressive and making mistakes early in points even though one of his strengths is extending points and using his speed to get in the opponent's head. Both players made choices to go away from their strengths and in the end, they didn't play their best in those matches.

4. Impose your game on the opponent

Building off of number 3, you want to use your strengths to impose your game style on the opponent. You have to make the other player fight your fight. When you do that, you'll feel more confident and in control of the match. The key component of this is knowing what your game is and how to play it at all times.

5. Keep it simple - 3 to 5 breaths between points

Overthinking can be a real problem for many tennis competitors while in a match because it tends to make the process more complex than it needs to be. One way to start to think less is to simply count your breaths between points. It takes your focus off of whatever is happening in the match and brings it to something you can consciously control - your breathing. 3 to 5 rhythmic breaths between points can truly simplify your approach and your focus. Your body knows how to play tennis and if you can focus more on your breath, you'll get your mind out of the body's way.

6. Use the actions of energy/intensity to change a match

This is a theme I discuss with all of my students. Lots of players are on an even-keel for most of a match, but there are moments in which you need to increase your focus and intensity. It might be at the end of a set or the match. It might be a break point. Whatever that moment is, you need to step it up. The question is how? It all starts with your energy. Get your feet moving. Bounce up and down. Use your self-talk to say "let's go", "c'mon" or some other motivating phrase. Keep it up for several points in a row and you'll notice a real difference. The result of this behavior will be increased intensity and focus. I have seen good results from players when they consciously do this in their matches.

7. Indoor tennis vs. outdoor tennis

A few years ago, a coaching friend of mine from Texas was in town to observe some players, and I asked him to compare players in New England to their counterparts in Texas. His first observation was the "shape" of the ball. Shape is a relatively common term in coaching circles and it refers to the trajectory of the ball off of a player's racquet to the other side of the court. He observed that the players in New England played with much less margin over the net, and that in Texas, a higher and heavier ball is the standard thus leading to longer, tougher points in general. It's likely that this is a key difference between indoor tennis and outdoor tennis. With no wind and fast courts, a high-risk game can be rewarded when playing indoors. However, the move to outdoors can be a huge change for some, as those shots that were winners indoors are now coming back into play. If you have more outdoor events coming up, be mindful of the patience and shape required to be successful.

8. Use simple reminders on-court

I often give each of my students an index card with 2 to 3 reminders for them to focus on for their tournaments. My goal is to help simplify the thought process on court to a few things. If they do those 2 to 3 things well, they should be happy with their performances. In general, this works well and the players like it. I urge you to have some reminders that you can use on the court during the change of sides so that you keep the thought process simple and on the right behaviors.

9. Your behavior between points matters

What you do between points not only indicates your level of mental toughness, but can also reflect your character as a person. For those players looking to play college tennis, be aware that any coach worth playing for will be paying attention to your behavior in between points. Sure, there will be some coaches who are blind to what happens between points and will be fixated on your play, but you don't want to be on those teams. What a good coach is looking for is someone who never stops fighting in a match, is respectful, and is composed in the big moments. Bring those behaviors to the court between points and you'll find that good college coaches will be interested in having you join their program.

10. "Hope for the best; plan for the worst"

Just a bit of good life advice here and in a tennis context, this is about being fully prepared for something that has the potential to distract you and stir up negative emotions. Excessive celebrations by the opponent, bad line calls, wind, etc. are all examples of distractions that could and often do occur in tennis matches. You have to go into a match expecting these things to happen and have a plan for what you are going to do when they occur. In the software world, this is what is called "If This, Then That" (IFTT). If this happens, then do that. "That" should consist of you taking some sort of action that displays taking control of the situation so that you remain focused on your objective. If someone makes consistently bad line calls, you need to have a plan for what you are going to do in that situation. Letting it distract you and getting emotional about it will only help the opponent.

Apply the lessons above and I guarantee you will compete better.

SECTION 3: FOCUS AND CONFIDENCE

41. CONFIDENCE

A vitally important ingredient to mental toughness and performing your best is confidence. I know that isn't exactly profound, but many athletes struggle with developing confidence so that they can compete at a high level consistently. We want to develop the kind of confidence that is unshakeable no matter the circumstances. In order to do this, let's focus on two high level concepts that factor into your confidence:

- Faith in yourself
- Trust in your abilities

If you look up the word faith in the dictionary, one of the definitions you'll find is "belief that is not based on proof." That is exactly the point I want to make. The greatest athletes, the greatest leaders, the greatest achievers in history have all had an unwavering faith in their ability to succeed, whether there was reason to believe or not. That's the key concept here as past performance does NOT have to be a predictor of future performance. Consider the following quote which I think is apropos in this case.

Faith is taking the first step even when you don't see the whole staircase.
-Martin Luther King, Jr.

The beginning of any journey toward a new goal requires you to get started without really knowing if you can do it, but you must believe that you can. You must believe that you can compete with anyone. You must believe that you can win against any opponent even if you've never defeated them before. Does this mean you'll always succeed or always win? No, of course it doesn't, but even if you don't succeed you will have learned and improved along the way. However, if you don't have this kind of faith, you'll never reach your potential, you'll never achieve the level of success you desire, and you'll never conquer those opponents who represent a challenge for you because you will have defeated yourself before you started.

Trust is different from faith in that it is evidence based and is more specific to your abilities. A concept I emphasize in my coaching practice is competing through your strengths because your best performances flow through your strengths. These are the parts of your game that define who you are as an athlete and competitor, and when under pressure it is these strengths that you have to trust so that you come through in the clutch. Great free throw shooters make free throws at the end of a close basketball game. Great quarterbacks make the sideline throw in the two-minute drill. Great tennis players make their best shots in a third set tiebreaker. These athletes have worked on these skills so much that they are automatic. Under pressure, they go to these skills and they trust them. There is no doubt. There is complete trust. Of course, having trust in your skills doesn't mean that you will always succeed, but it is better to play confidently through your strengths than it is to doubt your abilities and play it safe.

Work on building faith in yourself and trusting your abilities, and you will begin to know confidence as your good friend in competition.

42. ENCOURAGEMENT

It's amazing what a little encouragement can do for a competitor. A few years ago, I was playing a National tournament and I was in the locker room talking to a fellow player. I had just won a grueling match on clay in the Florida heat. My body was exhausted. My shoulder was screaming in pain. And my next match was going to be tough ... very tough. At that moment, I wasn't sure I was up for the competitive challenge. But then a funny thing happened.

That fellow player I was speaking with said I could win the match. We talked a bit more about the specific matchup, and the idea of winning started to come together in my mind. I began to visualize how it could happen. I saw myself competing with great intensity and confidence. I thought to myself, "if this guy thinks I can do it, then maybe I can!" At that moment, I committed myself to doing everything I could to win that match. I thanked him for his kind words of encouragement, and then used them for the rest of the day to visualize the kind of tennis I needed to play to be successful.

I am highlighting this brief exchange for a couple of reasons. Encouragement is a critical factor in confidence. As competitors, coaches, parents, etc., we shouldn't be afraid to give it. It is truly a gift to those on the receiving end. And it's a gift that the competitor needs to be willing to listen to and receive. Be open to it and do not dismiss it. Even if the encouragement seems irrational, it's always better to believe that you CAN do something rather than thinking you can't.

And to wrap up the story, I won the next day in a tough 3-hour match. It was one of the biggest wins of my tennis career. A few words of encouragement took me from a place where I wasn't sure I wanted to compete, to believing I could win, to actually pulling it off. That's a powerful transformation and a hugely satisfying one. Try spreading some encouragement today and see what powerful transformations you start to create.

43. PREPARE FOR SUCCESS

"Before anything else, preparation is the key to success."
-ALEXANDER GRAHAM BELL

Are you prepared to compete today? Have you done everything possible to get ready? If you answered yes to these questions, then you should feel confident going into your competition. However, if you're like most of us, your preparation could use some improvement. One of the issues with preparation is that it's not taught explicitly, and there are few systems for developing preparation routines except at the highest levels of athletic competition.

When thinking about how to best prepare, consider the following 4 training areas:

- Motivation
- Mental
- Emotional
- Physical

Motivation - Why are you competing? Do you know the answer to that question? Write it on a piece of paper and read it on a daily basis. Set some goals that help you achieve this motivation and connect with them daily. This will help you bring intensity and purpose to your performance on the day of competition.

Mental - Mental preparation is about focus and control. Focus only on the things that you can control. While you're competing, you want your mind to be quiet so that your body can perform at a peak level. To enable this, you need to be able to eliminate distractions. One way to handle distractions ahead of time is by writing down all of the possible distractions that could occur during a competition and formulating a proactive strategy for dealing with them. If something does happen, you'll be ready for it and able to regain your focus quickly.

Emotional - Emotional preparation is about Optimism and Confidence. I want to cultivate positivity and optimism into my approach to everything in life including my training. Specifically, I like to use guided visualization before I compete. This guided visualization is in the form of an audio recording that I created which induces progressive relaxation and then guides me through a performance. It gets me relaxed physically and in the right emotional state for competing at my best.

Physical - There are so many components to physical preparation: strength training, practice, diet, sleep, hydration, equipment, warm-up, etc. Some of these components are part of your overall training plan and some are more specific to what needs to be done prior to competing. Make sure you're considering all of these items so that you're physically ready. If you're not at your peak energy level, your performance will naturally suffer.

To be successful, you need to get good at preparation. Winging it doesn't work. However, good preparation takes practice and learning. See what works for you and what doesn't in preparation routines, and then adjust. Over time, you'll settle into a routine that regularly brings out your best. The prepared competitor ALWAYS has the advantage. Take advantage of the power of preparation and you shall be rewarded.

44. CHOOSE TO BE IN CONTROL

In order to be successful in life and in sports, there are two important concepts to understand and adopt: Choice and Control. How we react to a given situation is our choice. What we choose to focus on should be things that are under our control. There are times in life when these concepts get away from us and we let our emotions get the best of us.

As a coach, I like to promote and model ethical behavior with my students because I think acting that way demonstrates how I would like to be treated. Basically, that's the Golden Rule - treat others as you wish to be treated. Character traits such as respect, loyalty, integrity, honor, fairness, truthfulness and kindness are important to me, and I think they can be reflected in a sporting context. However, participation in sports does not automatically bring out these behaviors. As human beings, we learn through observation, imitation and modeling, and then we apply what we learn to various situations. Sports just give us a context for demonstrating what we've learned - good or bad.

Sometimes we are confronted with an opponent who does not act in a manner that we would consider to be ethical or proper. They may cheat, try to intentionally distract us, or perhaps verbally confront us in an effort to take us out of our game and have us react emotionally. And when we do react emotionally, we are doing exactly what our opponent wants us to do - making bad decisions.

So how do we handle these situations? We go back to Choice and Control, and make sure that we truly apply these concepts. If we honestly want to play well and win (see the chapter on Framework for Winning), we must choose to focus on what we can control. We can't control what our opponent says and does. We can only control our response, and that is our choice.

Here's some advice that I gave to someone recently who asked me about how to deal with verbal intimidation from another player:

"... a mental trick that I use is to tell myself that this person is afraid of me. He knows he can't beat me and he's desperate. He's trying any means possible to get me distracted. I choose not to react to him. I will continue to focus on my best performance and I will continue to be better than him. My performances are my reaction, and he can't beat me. When people do this kind of thing to me (trash talk, etc.), I just smile because I know how to handle it. They can't break me because my focus is too good. I'm tougher than they are."

A good way to plan your own reaction to these types of situation is to create a Mindset Plan. Take a piece of paper and create 4 columns. In the first column, describe the situation that bothers you (cheating opponent, verbal intimidation, etc.). In the second column, write about your normal reaction to this type of incident. Include your thoughts, feelings, emotions and behavior. In the third column, describe your preferred response. How do you want to respond in the future when this happens again? Most likely, it will happen again so be as detailed as possible when describing your new response. In the last column, come up with a word or phrase that will help you focus on your new preferred response.

Review this until your preferred response becomes your automatic response. This new automatic response should reflect an understanding of Choice and Control, and it should be consistent with your ethical character as a person. Do this well, and you'll always be proud of your efforts, win or lose.

45. FOCUS OVER A LONG PERIOD OF TIME

One of the challenges that many athletes face in competition is the ability to focus for long periods of time. Competitions can be long. They can be tiring. Perhaps there are a lot of distractions. Whatever the challenge is, we need a way to focus better.

Let's begin with some background. There are 4 dimensions to focus: Broad, Narrow, Internal, and External. We can combine them into Broad-Internal, Broad-External, Narrow-Internal and Narrow-External. While we are competing, we have various thoughts going through our head that could be categorized into these 4 combinations. For the purposes of this discussion, I'm more interested in the Broad versus Narrow distinction.

Broad Focus

To me, Broad Focus means that we're thinking about the competitive event as a whole. We're thinking about things like the significance of the event, winning, the overall score, etc. Basically, this is big picture thinking and it's absolutely necessary. Most of us are good at this kind of focus and many of our thoughts are on the big picture. Unfortunately, Broad Focus alone doesn't help us play our best and focusing at this level solely can get exhausting.

Narrow Focus

Almost every sport can be broken down into a set of discrete components and it's important that we as competitors understand that break down as that will help us establish our Narrow Focus. Let's look at a few sports and how we can break them down into components:

FOOTBALL
Football Game > 1st Half & 2nd Half > Each Half has 2 Quarters > Each Quarter has multiple possessions > Each possession has one or more plays

Going through this process shows us that in Football, the "play" is a very good discrete component that we can use for narrow focus. One could even break that down to six seconds at a time – the average length of time of a play.

TENNIS
Tennis Match > Has 2 or more sets > Each set has 6 to 13 games > Each game has 4 or more points

In tennis, our narrow focus is on the "point."

Here are some ideas for narrow focal points in other sports:

Basketball: Every possession of the ball and transition from offense to defense and defense to offense

Hockey: Every shift on the ice

Baseball: Every pitch

Other sports may be more difficult to do this, so you may have to create some artificial boundaries or components. For example, I worked with a marathon runner a few years ago and we decided to narrow his focus from a 26-mile race to

26 one-mile races. He focused on one mile at a time and set a personal best.

The reason we want to understand this discrete component is because that is the level in which we can actually exert control over our performance. Understanding what you can control is a major part of being a great competitor, and we want to get our best performance at each play, point, etc.

Getting to this narrow focal point is only half the battle. In order to improve our ability to focus at this level, rather than just broadly, we need to add routines around the focal point. We need to do the same things all the time on those plays, points, pitches, etc. What we do in between these plays, points, pitches is one of the keys to being mentally tough. Here is an example of what I do on the tennis court:

> *"When a point ends, I immediately focus on two things: my body language and my breathing. I want my body language to display a confident, strong, fighting image. I focus on my breath to help recover from the last point. I always have a towel at the back of the court and I go there to use it whether it's truly necessary or not. At some point in my walk to the towel or back to the baseline, I press the vibration dampener in my strings as my "Reset Button". It's a key component of my routine. I need to completely reset myself (mentally and emotionally) for the next point and I have found that doing something physically like pressing a button makes this work even better. The next point is the most important one now and I want to play my best. As I walk to get into position, I'm still reflecting great body language and I'm visualizing my best tennis. I know that the more great points I play, the more likely that I'm going to get the result I want so I've trained myself to be good at narrow focus."*

To make this really simple: Point – Reset – Point – Reset – Point – Reset, etc. The same goes for every other sport and its narrow focal point. This adds up to a great overall performance.

Enacting this kind of routine in your sport will take time. It will require some additional focus energy at first, but keep doing it. The more you do it, the more automatic it will become. And once your routine is automatic, you will find it much easier to focus for long periods throughout the course of your competitive event.

46. A NEW PRIMARY GOAL WHEN YOU COMPETE

If you play a sport in which you or your team has a direct opponent that you are competing against (football, basketball, soccer, hockey, tennis, etc.), what is your primary goal when you start playing? Is it to win? Is it to execute your game plan or do your job? Is it to play well? Perhaps it's something else? These are all valid perspectives, but let me give you a new one to consider. One that may make you re-examine your other perspectives and how you actually perform them.

Your primary goal when you compete is to break your opponent mentally. Yes, you read that correctly. I want you to focus on breaking your opponent mentally. Everything you do should be with this goal in mind. Your game plan, how you attack your opponent, how you manage your body language and self-talk, your confidence, etc. – all of these things must contribute to the breaking of your opponent. This is the ultimate lesson in becoming a great competitor and once you do it for the first time, you'll realize that you've moved to a new level. It is the pinnacle of competition.

To some of you, this may sound a little cruel, but the fact of the matter is you're more or less doing this already. You're just not as focused on it as you should be. And you're not looking for the signs of it happening enough either. If you were, you wouldn't be making some of the mistakes that you're making today that allow your opponents to stay in the game longer than they should. Why do we focus on this? Because when your opponent breaks mentally, they quit competing. They stop trying and they make it easier for you to win.

How do you break your opponents mentally? There are a couple of ways that I want to highlight. First is pressure. Your game plan or your style of play must somehow exert pressure on your opponent. It must make them uncomfortable in some way. It must take them out of their game and put them in your game. When competitors feel pressure, they can start to make poor decisions. They may try to do things that they can't really do well because their normal game has no answer for what you are doing to them. I want you to examine your style of play or your game plan and really understand how it is putting pressure on the opponent. How does your game plan make them uncomfortable? If you're not making opponents uncomfortable, you're not going to be successful.

Second is own the critical moments. In a previous chapter, I wrote about how to succeed in the critical moments, and the more you do this, the more your opponent is going to break. They are going to be frustrated and angry, and that will give you the advantage. I see this in tennis all the time. If one player is winning more of the deuce games in a match, that eventually gets into his/her opponent's head.

The last method is somewhat related to the first and it is that you try to break your opponent's physical conditioning. Nothing breaks the will to compete like fatigue, and if you can exhaust your opponent, they'll start making mistakes and they'll check out mentally. Early in the competition, show your opponent how hard they are going to have to work to earn the victory, and you may find that they aren't up for it. The physical exhaustion will lead to mental fatigue and that will lead to you coming out on top.

Once you start to compete with this goal in mind, you must also be observant of the signs of a mentally breaking opponent: anger, frustration, complaining, arguing, bad body language, low energy, lack of effort, poor decision making, etc. When you see these behaviors, don't let them upset you. Be happy about it. This is exactly what you want, and once you start seeing some of these things, it's your job to make sure your opponent keeps acting this way. Don't do anything that might reinstate their confidence or help them get back in the fight.

Before we conclude, let's discuss some things that you should not do to break your opponents mentally: cheating, taunting, intimidation, deliberate confrontation, and other unethical means. These are not the methods of great competitors. They are for cowards and for people who don't have the courage to put their abilities on the line. Winning through these methods is an empty experience and will never be completely fulfilling, so don't use them when trying to break your opponent mentally.

How you use your game, your strategy, your conditioning, your body language and your thoughts is plenty when it comes to breaking your opponent mentally. This concept has had a tremendous impact on my ability to compete and has helped me to focus my efforts with greater purpose.

47. STAY FOCUSED ON WINNING

There are many thoughts that go through an athlete's mind while competing. Some are beneficial, and others are not. To compete well, the athlete has to be able to separate the productive thoughts from the destructive ones.

A perspective that I use is that all of my energy, both mental and physical, should be in the direction of helping me win. That's the mission. Otherwise, I'm wasting my time and energy. If I focus on the wrong things, I'm probably going to underperform. The list below shows a few things that don't help you win and are generally a waste of energy:

- Getting angry
- Excessive celebrations
- Taunting your opponent or fans
- Arguing with opponents or officials

Instead of focusing your energy on things that are not beneficial and are just distractions, begin to distinguish between what you can control and what you cannot control. Ask yourself, "Is this helping me win?" Or think about WIN: What's Important Now. Put your energy into those things that you can control and help you perform better. If you perform better, you have a better chance of winning. Right? Here are some suggestions:

- Your thoughts - keep them optimistic and positive
- Body Language - reflect a strong, confident and positive image

- Breathing - deep breathing to get your heart rate down
- Routines/Rituals - stick to what works so that you take your time and perform at a comfortable pace

It will take some discipline and practice to focus only on what you can control as many of us have used distractions as excuses for poor performances for a long time, but once you learn this skill, it will be tremendously empowering. Commit to being 100% focused on what helps you perform better and win because if it's not helping you win, why are you doing it?

48. THE TWO TYPES OF BELIEF THAT YOU NEED TO BE MENTALLY TOUGH

When discussing mental toughness, everyone talks about confidence and how important it is. But what about self-belief? Is that important? It turns out that it is. Let's examine self-belief more deeply because it may not be apparent that there are two types of self-belief that are critical to be a mentally tough competitor (Jones, Hanton, & Connaughton, 2002). They are:

1. Belief that you can achieve your competitive goals
2. Belief that you possess unique qualities and abilities that make you better than your opponents

Belief that you can achieve your competitive goals

This belief might seem obvious, but the difference is that this belief is an **unshakable** belief. Doubt may creep in every now and then, but it never derails you. You always believe that you can do what you have set out to do. I have often written of the necessity of optimism in being a great competitor, and this is a major reason why. You can't achieve your competitive goals if you're not an optimist, and optimism is the beginning of the path to creating that unshakable belief in your mind. No matter what happens, you need to know that you will achieve your goals. That's total optimism.

It's possible that you don't have that unshakable belief today. So how can you start to develop it? Use these steps to get started:

1. Write down your competitive goal(s)
2. Write down the process goals and actions necessary to achieve your competitive goal
3. Take action everyday
4. Review your progress weekly and monthly
5. Develop an optimistic mindset (gratitude journal, reframing exercises, etc.)
6. Look for sources of inspiration and review them weekly

If you can stick to these action steps (especially steps 3 and 4), you'll be on your way to establishing that unshakable belief you need to achieve your competitive goal.

Belief in your unique qualities and abilities

This type of self-belief is a key attribute of the mentally tough competitor. Every great competitor believes that there is something unique that separates him/her from others. This is also an unshakable belief. It could be a technical skill. It could be strength or fitness. It could be something mental like perseverance. It could be the ability to perform under pressure. Perhaps it's something like "I always win the close matches/games/competitions, etc." We all have unique qualities that make us great and differentiate us from others. What's your unique quality or ability? What are you better at than the rest of your competitors? Don't know? Use the following to help figure out your special ingredient:

1. Write down a list of your strengths as a competitor – be sure to consider more than just your physical skills

2. Think about how you have used those strengths in your best performances
3. Write down how those strengths can make your opponents uncomfortable
4. Based on this, which strength is your special ingredient?

If you still can't pinpoint your unique ability, watch your favorite athletes and see if you can identify what makes them so uniquely great. Maybe they do something that you want to do too. If so, start acting/competing like that is your special quality. Make it a strength of yours and use it often. Remind yourself of what makes you different and bring that knowledge with you everywhere you go to compete. When you get in a tight situation, use that unique ability to help you succeed.

Being mentally tough requires confidence and self-belief. Develop unshakable belief in your ability to achieve your competitive goals and in your unique qualities as a competitor, and you'll be well on the path to becoming a great competitor.

References

Jones, G., Hanton, S., & Connaughton, D. (2002). What is this thing called mental toughness? An investigation of elite sport performers. *Journal of Applied Sport Psychology*, 14. 205 - 218.

49. USE YOUR VOICE TO BOOST YOUR CONFIDENCE

Confidence is a choice. However, many athletes choose not to be confident and therefore make the road to good performance more difficult. Confidence and Mental Toughness are actions which then create feelings and thoughts. I teach athletes to use their bodies to express power and confidence through their posture and their walk. This very simple intervention works. This helps them choose to be confident. There is another simple action you can take to get a confidence boost: Use your voice and your words.

Your tone of voice and the language you use reflects your state of mind. Athletes who lack confidence tend to speak more softly during competition or not at all. The words come from their throat rather than their abdomen. You can see this in young tennis players before a point when they are supposed to call out the score. For various reasons, some players don't call out the score before a point and that's a mistake. It could be due to a lack of confidence or it might be peer pressure driving this behavior as many players don't say the score. Whatever it is, it's a lost opportunity. The moment in which you call out the score is an opportunity to establish your presence and assertiveness on the court, and boost your confidence. When you call out the score, do it loudly and definitively. Speak from your abdomen (diaphragm). You will feel in control of the situation. This kind of communication will also show your opponent that you are confident.

This also applies to team sports. A few years ago, I worked with a Division 1 volleyball program and we talked about using our voices as one of our competitive tools to establish presence, confidence and assertiveness. During the final weekend of their season, the team noticed that they were louder than their opponents, especially as the game went along. They also noticed that when they got a little quiet, they didn't play as well. For them, communication and voice were a key ingredient in performing well. When the opponents got quiet, they knew they were starting to break mentally.

No matter what was going on in the game, our team stayed loud, which kept them engaged and focused. Their final two performances that season were great displays of mental toughness and their voices made it happen. They broke their opponents mentally and the best part is that the team saw it. That is the pinnacle of mental toughness.

Look to use your voice to establish presence and confidence before you compete and during the game. You will feel better and more confident, and your opponents will know that they can't break you. You can choose to be confident by choosing to use your voice as a tool in your mental toughness toolbox.

50. THREE THINGS TO REMEMBER WHEN YOU ARE ON TOP OF YOUR GAME

You're having a great season. You're playing well, the victories are piling up and you've never felt better about your game. And of course, you want this feeling to last for as long as possible. In order to keep things going as they are, use the following 3 points as a guide for keeping yourself on track.

1. Continue the discipline - You haven't reached this position without working hard and being disciplined in your approach. Whether you realize it or not, that's a major reason as to why you're so successful. Continue to do what you're doing, and continually look for new habits and routines that will make you better. Oftentimes, success can lead us to get a little lazy about our routines and we have to guard against that. That's self-sabotage. Don't fall prey to this. Understand that your success is determined by your daily agenda so keep it focused and committed to achieving your best.

2. Know who is in your corner - Everyone notices a successful team and/or athlete. People want to be associated with them. They want to hang out with them. However, these people don't always have your best interests in mind when they come into your lives. They may distract you. They may tell you that you should be getting more playing time. They may tell you that they will make you rich. Their influence can be destructive and divisive, and ultimately may lead to a major drop in performance. Always remember who helped you become successful: your family, your teammates, your coaches and trainers, your long-time friends. When success comes, it's important that you express gratitude to these people and strengthen your bonds with them. If new people are to come into your circle, let your "team" help you make the decision that these new people right for you.

3. Be humble and respectful - Just because your successful right now, doesn't mean you always will be. You came from nothing and you can always go back to being nothing if you're not careful. How you conduct yourself and how you treat other people matters. Be humble and gracious. Your talent doesn't make you better than everyone else. Realize that hard work is what transforms talent into success and if you don't work hard, your success will disappear a lot faster than it appeared. Respect those around you and build great relationships with them. At the end of your life, the ledger of success isn't quantified in victories on the court or field. It's based on the number of lives you've touched, influenced and helped. Use your success in sport to be a success outside of it.

We all want to be successful throughout our lives, but we often sabotage ourselves. Almost every day, you can read a story about a celebrity or athlete who has fallen from grace. These are cautionary tales and we should pay attention to them. However, even if we do fall down, nothing is permanent. You became successful once and you can do it again. Just remember how you got there and understand how you can stay there. I wish you much success!

About the Author

Brian Lomax is an expert in training mental skills and is the creator of the PerformanceXtra training program. He has consulted for numerous athletic teams and athletes at institutions such as Brown University, Bryant University, Holy Cross College, Boston College, University of Rhode Island, and Regis College. He is also the mental skills trainer for the New England Academy of Tennis. Brian's private students have enjoyed success at local, collegiate and national levels in a variety of sports including tennis, golf, football, volleyball, basketball, softball, field hockey, and figure skating. Through the PerformanceXtra training program, his students have not only become better competitors, but they have also learned the character skills necessary for leading a fulfilling life.

A competitive tennis player since the age of 8, Brian transformed his own mental game in his 30's and achieved a career best ranking of #2 in the US in the Men's 35 and over singles category. In 2010, he left a successful corporate career to start his own mental toughness coaching business - PerformanceXtra. For more information about Brian and his products and services, visit http://www.performancextra.com.

Made in the USA
Middletown, DE
10 August 2021

45747833R00085